# Luftwaffe
## *over*
# Scotland

A HISTORY OF GERMAN AIR ATTACKS ON
SCOTLAND 1939–1945

*Les Taylor*

W

Whittles Publishing

**To my family
Glenda, Gavin and Kerry**

*Published by*
**Whittles Publishing,**
Dunbeath,
Caithness KW6 6EY,
Scotland, UK

www.whittlespublishing.com

Text, illustrations and maps © 2010 Les Taylor

ISBN 978-184995-000-8

Every effort has been made by the author to verify the accuracy of the information
presented; to trace copyright holders and to obtain their permission for the use of
copyright material. The publisher would be grateful if notified of any amendments
that should be incorporated in future reprints or editions of this book.

Printed and bound in the United Kingdom
by the Charlesworth Group, Wakefield

# CONTENTS

# Locations where bombs were dropped in Scotland

| Multiple attacks | Bombed once only | Bombed once only |
|---|---|---|
| 1. Peterhead = 28 | 41. Anstruther | 81. Perth |
| 2. Aberdeen = 24 | 42. Armadale | 82. Pittenweem |
| 3. Fraserburgh = 23 | 43. Auchterless | 83. Portknockie |
| 4. Edinburgh = 18 | 44. Auchtermuchty | 84. Sanquhar |
| 5. Montrose = 15 | 45. Ayr | 85. Sauchie |
| 6. Glasgow = 11 | 46. Banffshire | 86. St Fergus |
| 7. Dundee = 7 | 47. Berwickshire | 87. Tobermory |
| 8. Orkney = 7 | 48. Bonnybridge | 88. Thurso |
| 9. Shetland = 7 | 49. Broxburn | 89. Wishaw |
| 10. Wick = 6 | 50. Bucksburn | |
| 11. Greenock = 5 | 51. Burntisland | |
| 12. Banff = 4 | 52. Coatbridge | |
| 13. Dunfermline = 4 | 53. Coldstream | |
| 14. Firth of Forth = 4 | 54. Cowdenbeath | |
| 15. Gourock = 4 | 55. Cullen | |
| 16. Rosehearty = 4 | 56. Cupar | |
| 17. Clydebank = 3 | 57. Drem | |
| 18. Crail = 3 | 58. Duns | |
| 19. Cumbernauld = 3 | 59. East Linton | |
| 20. Haddington = 3 | 60. Edzell | |
| 21. Invergordon = 3 | 61. Elie | |
| 22. Newburgh = 3 | 62. Falkland | |
| 23. North Berwick = 3 | 63. Foyers | |
| 24. Aberdeenshire = 2 | 64. Glenkindie | |
| 25. Arbroath = 2 | 65. Greenlaw | |
| 26. Ardeer = 2 | 66. Gretna | |
| 27. Campbeltown = 2 | 67. Guardbridge | |
| 28. Cruden bay = 2 | 68. Helensburgh | |
| 29. Dumbarton = 2 | 69. Hillington | |
| 30. Dunbar = 2 | 70. Innerwick | |
| 31. Eyemouth = 2 | 71. Kilmarnock | |
| 32. Fort William = 2 | 72. Kincardineshire | |
| 33. Kelty = 2 | 73. Kinglassie | |
| 34. Loch Ewe = 2 | 74. Kirkconnel | |
| 35. Lossiemouth = 2 | 75. Larbert | |
| 36. Portlethen = 2 | 76. Moffat | |
| 37. Portsoy = 2 | 77. Monifieth | |
| 38. Renfrew = 2 | 78. Motherwell | |
| 39. St Andrews = 2 | 79. Oban | |
| 40. Stirling = 2 | 80. Paisley | |

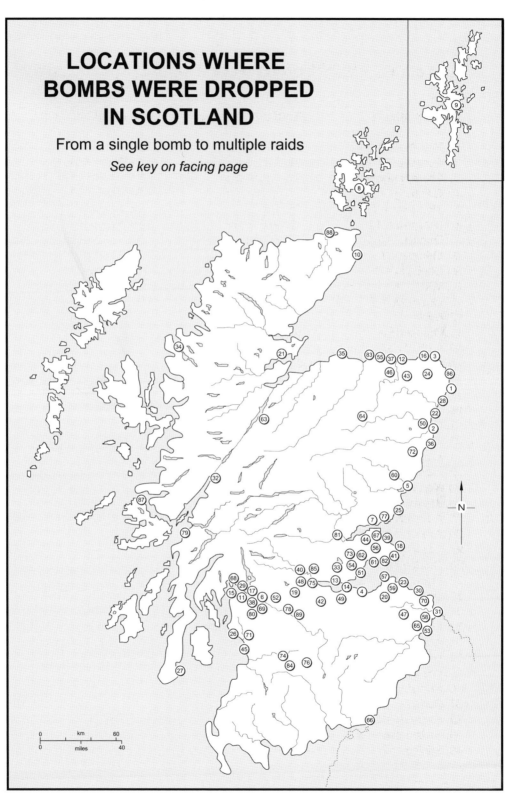

# LOCATIONS WHERE BOMBS WERE DROPPED IN SCOTLAND

From a single bomb to multiple raids

*See key on facing page*

# THE DOUHET THEORY

In the years before the Second World War began, the relatively new weapon of air bombardment was a subject of fierce debate around the world. Indications of what fleets of bomber aircraft could do to a city had been given during the First World War, when German Gotha bombers and Zeppelin airships raided Britain. This terrible new strategic weapon shocked people because it implied that innocent civilians were to be considered legitimate targets in any future war. Nobody would be safe. Arguments raged not only about whether bombing was an effective method of waging war, but also about the morality of it. One man, however, seemed to settle the debate. He was Giulio Douhet, an Italian General and a dedicated advocate of the use of modern air power. His 1921 book *The Command of the Air* became standard reading at military staff colleges around the world and his ideas became accepted as the way forward.

The maxim was simple: The bomber will always get through.

Douhet's central theory was particularly controversial, however. He claimed that the bomber offered an alternative to the traditional method of waging war on battlefields. Coming so soon after the appalling carnage in the trenches of Flanders, this was precisely what military commanders wanted to hear. The deliberate and repeated bombing of civilian populations, Douhet claimed, would bring about a collapse in the morale of the people subjected to such attacks. He predicted that they would rise up en masse against their governments and demand an immediate end to the war, even if that meant surrendering. It seemed a logical if very cruel argument, but one that ignored the fact that this attempt to avoid carnage in the trenches would simply produce carnage in the streets. The only counter to an enemy equipped with a massive strategic bomber fleet, it was argued, would be to build a similarly large bomber fleet to act as a deterrent. Others argued that the best defence against bombers would be an equally massive fleet of fighter aircraft to shoot down the bombers. Each side believed they were right, although each knew that the only way their theories could be proved would be in a real war, which was unfortunate, since the guinea pigs in this great military experiment would be innocent civilians in the towns and cities that were to be attacked.

Forward-thinking nations prepared. Bomb shelters and air-raid precautions were put in place. The fear of what bombing could do was very real, and that fear was soon justified by an event that took place in 1937 during the Spanish Civil War. In April that year, a small force of only twenty-eight German medium bomber aircraft attacked the Republican-held town of Guernica in the Basque region and virtually wiped it out. While the true figure of civilian deaths in Guernica was subject to the vagaries of propaganda from each side at the time, ranging from a realistic 250 to an unrealistic 1,600 deaths, one thing that was never in dispute was the awful totality of the destruction inflicted on the town. The world saw the pictures in their newspapers and on cinema newsreels and knew that Douhet's terrible theory looked as if it might well be proven if practised on a bigger scale. With Nazi Germany rattling sabres in central Europe, most people felt that this vision of Armageddon might not be too far away. And they were right. In each of the future combatant nations, two influential devotees of the Douhet doctrine, one in Britain and one in Germany, were to have a massive impact on the course of that war, for very different reasons.

The first was a German general named Walter Wever. Tasked with building the new Luftwaffe, Wever specifically set out to create the new German air force as a strategic, long-range heavy bomber force along the lines of the Douhet principle. Consequently, the first modern four-engine heavy bombers, aircraft like the superb Junkers Ju-89, began to undergo air testing in Germany long before any other nation had even decided upon the need for heavy bombers. Wever publicly declared that for Germany to enter any future war with anything less would be 'madness'. But Germany did end up going to war with considerably less than Wever intended. When Wever was killed in a flying accident in 1936, his place was taken by Albert Kesselring, a very talented former soldier but one who, like his superior Hermann Göring, had no interest in the Douhet theory. Kesselring immediately cancelled the entire German heavy bomber programme at a stroke, simply because he knew that bigger numbers of smaller tactical bombers could be built more quickly and cheaply than expensive heavy bombers, and besides, everyone knew that Adolf Hitler much preferred to hear about big numbers. In retrospect, it was clearly a very bad decision.

Some historians go so far as to claim that this far-reaching decision by Kesselring effectively decided the outcome of the Second World War even before it had begun, for reasons we'll see.

In Britain the greatest exponent of the Douhet theory was a career officer in the Royal Air Force named Arthur Harris. When he was made head of RAF Bomber Command early in 1942, he began a programme that would revolutionise his force and eventually lay waste to most of Germany's cities. Like Wever, Harris also knew that he needed heavy four-engine bombers, and lots of them, in order to carry the maximum amount of high-explosives all the way to Germany's furthest cities. He never got the five thousand bombers he demanded, but even with the force he did have, he began to mount spectacular thousand-bomber raids on Germany that grabbed headlines all over the world. So confident was Harris that he and Douhet were right, that he famously (and rashly) predicted that his bomber force would alone defeat Germany. But Harris and Douhet were wrong, as the people of Britain had already demonstrated. During the Blitz of 1940–41, the morale of the British people bent under the weight of German bombs, but did not completely break. Neither would that of the German people, who were to face far greater death and devastation all across their nation than anything seen in Britain.

For almost six years, hundreds of thousands of people were required to die in the bombed cities of the world in order to disprove a flawed military theory. And in every city that was attacked, it was the working-class people who always suffered most, because almost without exception they were crammed into row after row of poor quality housing where one hit could kill hundreds. But this was the whole point of the Douhet policy. Perhaps uniquely in the history of war, the strategy was a deliberately class-based one. Harris, for all his shortcomings, was at least honest about this. One clearly stated aim of his area-bombing policy of German cities was that of 'dehousing' workers in the key armaments industries. He knew that huge swathes of working-class housing districts were far easier to hit than the factory buildings that these workers were employed in. An undamaged factory full of lathes is useless if the skilled lathe operators have all been killed, wounded or rendered homeless and distressed.

An obvious factor preventing the intended revolt of the bombed-out working classes in Germany was the totalitarian nature of the Nazi regime, which ruthlessly suppressed any hint of insurrection among the populace. This was not the case in Britain, and is the reason why the Douhet theory came closest to fulfilment in the East End of London. Bombed relentlessly during the Blitz of 1940–41 while other more affluent areas of London remained undamaged, the working-class East End in fact came very close to open revolt before, with almost impeccable timing, Buckingham Palace was hit by a bomb. Tuned in to the reality of the moment, the Queen famously declared that at least now she could 'look the East End in the eye'.

Much was made of the damage to the palace in the press and as a result the situation in the East End was quickly defused. As history clearly shows, Winston Churchill could be a cold and ruthless manipulator of events in those darkest hours of war, and one could easily be forgiven for speculating whether the bomb that hit the palace that night was a German one or a British one.

Nonetheless, Douhet was defeated in London, as he would be everywhere else in the world where his theory was tried out. Contrary to what some people claim, Douhet was not proved right with the atomic attacks on Hiroshima and Nagasaki either. In Japan it was the emperor's morale, not the morale of his people, that finally cracked and made him seek peace.

But Douhet was right about one thing. His declaration that the bomber would always get through was on the whole, pretty much true. There were only a few occasions in the Second World War when a force of bombers did not get all the way through to the target they had set out for (one of them will be dealt with later in this book), even if the results of those that did get through did not achieve the effects that Douhet and Harris had predicted. Until men like Harris were prepared to concede they were wrong, bomber crews from each of the combatant nations would continue to be sent out to prove a theory by deliberately killing civilians on the ground, even if the war was increasingly looking like a lost cause for Germany.

The Douhet theory was tried out in anger on many famous occasions and on many towns and cities across Europe. It is important that each generation is made aware what happened at these places, as well as why. For that reason, this book sets out to record how the Douhet theory was practised specifically in Scotland by the German Luftwaffe during the Second World War. No complete account of the bombing of Scotland between 1939 and 1945 exists, and I felt it was time that a single source of reference be produced to record this important period in the history of the modern Scottish nation.

In setting out to tackle this project, I decided to establish a few restricting parameters in order to limit the size of the finished publication. The first was that this be a reference book dealing only with facts and figures – what happened, where and when – rather than a collection of personal memoirs and experiences of the people who suffered under the bombing, because this is a subject already well covered in many excellent Scottish books. The second rule was that only verifiable information be included, no matter how good some local legends and anecdotes might be – although one or two exceptions are made.

Instead of attempting to describe every event, I provide tabulated lists of bombed locations together with relevant dates, as well as Scottish casualty lists and German aircraft losses over Scotland. Only the more notable events are dealt with in the narrative, it being an unrealistic proposition to describe every single incident of the war without the finished book resembling the size of a doorstep. Fortunately, because the majority of single hit-and-run raids in Scotland caused little or no damage or casualties, they need not all be individually described at any length in the narrative anyway.

One further point about what went into the narrative and what didn't is the importance of viewing wartime events as one complete picture. Looking at bombing attacks in isolation does not give this picture, and so in order to show how it must have felt to have been overwhelmed with momentous events on an almost daily basis, I include details of aspects such as the many U-boat sinkings that took place close inshore around Scotland's coasts. For instance, in the context of the first air attack on Britain at Rosyth in 1939, it is important to be aware that this happened two days after, and directly because of, the sinking of HMS *Royal Oak* at Scapa Flow in the Orkney Islands. The bombing attacks were simply one major aspect of the war in Scotland.

Another important consideration was that the book should be a relatively impartial account of these events. I feel it is essential to try to avoid the sort of emotive wartime language which, after more than sixty years, can surely be dispensed with in an objective contemporary account, and to stick to (or at least try to stick to) a neutral narrative style in order to achieve a degree of balance and perspective. That's why there are no 'Nazi' planes or pilots in this book, only German ones, even if they do not entirely escape criticism.

The attacks these German aircraft launched against Scotland reached a peak in 1940 and into the first half of 1941. Then the German invasion of the Soviet Union began to suck in most of the Luftwaffe's resources. Random attacks on Scotland continued in 1942, although on a much-reduced scale. A few short raids on the north-east corner brought an end to German air raids in the spring of 1943. Attacks still continued but by then the RAF had become a potent force in northern Scotland, totally dominating the skies to the extent that no more raids got through. It was clear that the worst of the bombing was over.

A final calculation of the bombing casualties in Scotland during the Second World War can never be considered exact, and must always be viewed allowing a good margin for error in either direction. The generally accepted figures of casualties in Scotland caused by German bombing between the years 1939 and 1945 are given as 2,298 people killed, 2,167 seriously injured and 3,558 slightly injured.

These figures need updating. They came from a press release issued by St Andrew's House in Edinburgh entitled *Scotland Under Fire* and dated 13 October 1944, which summarises the bombing in Scotland up to the end of 1942. In the absence of any further post-war material to go on, these statistics have become accepted as the final war tally of casualties in Scotland. But because they were produced before the war actually ended they must be considered incomplete. Furthermore, it is clear from the scarce post-war municipal records that do exist, that this 1944 report erred very much on the side of caution in terms of numbers killed, undoubtedly for the purposes of morale. For instance, the report quotes approximately 1,000 people killed in the Clydebank raids, when a compilation of post-war records provides a figure of at least 1,300 killed (over 500 in Clydebank and 800 in Glasgow).

Adding in the few remaining deaths in Scotland not covered by the report, as well as the increased numbers identified in post-war analyses, takes the number killed in Scotland by German air attack over the 2,500 mark. It is worth noting that these figures represent only the actual deaths recorded *at the time* of each particular incident. They do not take into account the near-certainty that a percentage of those listed as injured would inevitably have succumbed to their injuries and died as a direct result of a bombing incident either days, weeks, months or even, perhaps, years after the event. What that percentage was is something we'll never really know for sure, but the fact that more than two thousand people in Scotland were so seriously injured as to require hospitalisation for an unspecified period, and that a further 3,558 people were officially classified as 'slightly injured', tells its own story of misery and suffering.

One thing that is clear is that the vast majority of these casualties occurred during the concentrated two-night raid on Clydebank in March 1941 and also at Greenock a couple of months later. Although the material damage was so bad in Clydebank that the raids are always known as the 'Clydebank Blitz', nearly twice as many people were actually killed in Glasgow as were killed in Clydebank on these two nights, for reasons that will be revealed and explained for the first time in this book.

The bulk of the remaining Scottish wartime casualties were inflicted around the north-east coast, where Aberdeen was tormented relentlessly by hit-and-run raiders and the Peterhead-to-Fraserburgh areas were attacked so often that they earned the unwelcome nickname of Hellfire Corner.

Aberdeen has always been bestowed with the dubious honour of being the most frequently raided place in Scotland, with published figures usually quoting 34 individual attacks on the city. In reality, however, a close examination of Aberdeen's own archives reveal that the city was subjected to 24 *actual* bombing attacks during the war. Several factors unwittingly conspired to produce the inflated figure. German acoustic anti-shipping mines drifting ashore and exploding near Aberdeen beach were sometimes recorded as air raids. Furthermore, several raids were plotted approaching Aberdeen only for them to veer off towards other targets, yet these were still sometimes recorded as raids on the city.

The most frequently raided place in Scotland was actually Peterhead, which suffered a total of 28 separate air attacks, although sadly the town itself holds no archive records of these momentous events in its history. Fraserburgh was not far behind at 23 raids, although if the four attacks on nearby Rosehearty are included,

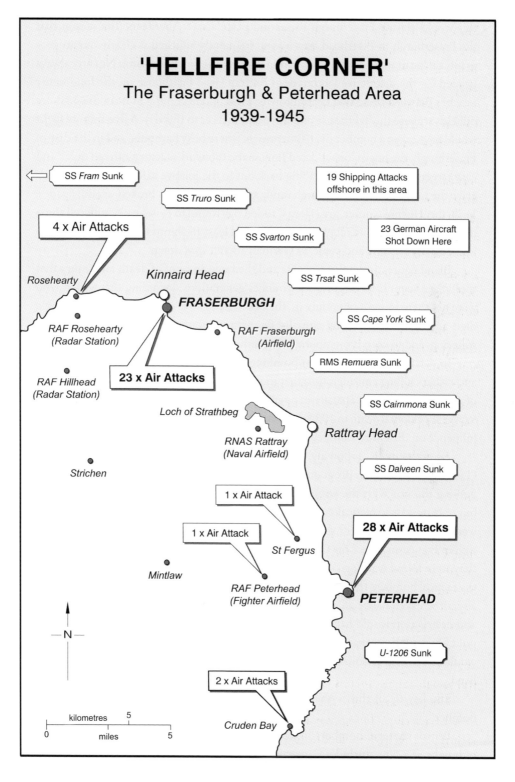

# 'HELLFIRE CORNER'
## The Fraserburgh & Peterhead Area
### 1939-1945

SS *Fram* Sunk

19 Shipping Attacks
offshore in this area

SS *Truro* Sunk

4 x Air Attacks

SS *Svarton* Sunk

23 German Aircraft
Shot Down Here

Rosehearty

Kinnaird Head

SS *Trsat* Sunk

**FRASERBURGH**

RAF Rosehearty
(Radar Station)

RAF Fraserburgh
(Airfield)

SS *Cape York* Sunk

RMS *Remuera* Sunk

**23 x Air Attacks**

RAF Hillhead
(Radar Station)

Loch of Strathbeg

SS *Cairnmona* Sunk

RNAS Rattray
(Naval Airfield)

Rattray Head

Strichen

SS *Dalveen* Sunk

1 x Air Attack

1 x Air Attack

**28 x Air Attacks**

St Fergus

Mintlaw

RAF Peterhead
(Fighter Airfield)

**PETERHEAD**

—N—

U-1206 Sunk

2 x Air Attacks

kilometres    5

0        miles        5

Cruden Bay

this would elevate Fraserburgh to second place above Aberdeen. The reason that the Fraserburgh-to-Peterhead area was so frequently attacked is clearly due to geographical location. Enemy aircraft coming in over the North Sea from Norway always headed for the distinctive landmark of Rattray Head lighthouse on the long sandy beaches between these two coastal towns. Helicopters coming in from the offshore oilfields still use the lighthouse as a waypoint marker to this day. A five-minute flight would have taken a bomber over either town, where busy harbours, and in the case of Fraserburgh, the huge Consolidated Pneumatic toolworks factory, offered quick and easy targets to bomb before heading back out to the relative safety of the sea. Ironically, the tool works at Fraserburgh rarely suffered more than broken window panes. In all, the 'Hellfire Corner' area from Cruden Bay round to Rosehearty suffered some 60 separate bombing incidents onshore, with at least 19 shipping attacks taking place immediately offshore and some 23 German aircraft shot down.

Bland figures aside, these events and the huge amount of death and injury that took place seem hard to grasp for younger generations, including this writer, who were not there to see it or endure it. The best we can do is recognise that every single digit among these appalling casualty figures represents a tale of human pain and suffering, and to keep remembering that it did happen, right here in Scotland.

In dealing with the German bombing of Scotland, however, there is one final and rather chilling consideration that must be made in order to provide a real sense of perspective to what actually happened. To do this we need to return to General Wever's accidental death in 1936 and examine precisely why this had such a profound influence on the entire European war.

As we've seen, following Wever's demise Kesselring cancelled the entire German heavy bomber programme. Put simply, this meant that Germany ended up fighting the war with the wrong kind of bombers. She needed strategic bombers, but only possessed tactical ones like the Heinkel He-111 and Dornier Do-17. These were excellent aircraft for short-range close battlefield support, as they proved so well in France and the Low Countries. Against distant targets like Britain, however, they were found wanting. Kesselring and Göring had backed the wrong horse and the tactical bombers they were stuck with were not up to the job. Even though these aircraft wreaked havoc all over Britain, this hides the reality that the scale of death and destruction would have been so much worse, possibly decisively so, if Wever's policy had not been abandoned. A huge fleet of powerful German strategic bombers would have been in squadron service by the outbreak of war in 1939, had Wever lived.

The key to all this is the basic difference between a tactical and a strategic bomber.

British strategic bombers like the Avro Lancaster could carry up to ten tons of bombs at a time, including huge 4,000-pounder 'Cookies', 8,000-pounders, and even ten-ton (22,000 lb) earthquake bombs, and they could carry them all the way across the Third Reich. The average German tactical bomber, by contrast, struggled to carry as much as a couple of tons of relatively small bombs to distant targets like Scotland.

This difference in aircraft capabilities made an enormous difference to the war. It meant that the Luftwaffe simply could not deliver anything like the huge, devastating blows that the Allies could.

Scotland's wartime bombing casualties totalled just over 8,000 deaths and injuries, yet Allied heavy bombers caused some 45,000 deaths – not casualties, *deaths* – in Hamburg alone in July 1943. In Tokyo two years later, even at a modest estimate, some 125,000 deaths were inflicted upon the civilian population by American B-29 Superfortress bombers dropping incendiaries.

These two individual attacks are mentioned here because they both resulted in a *firestorm* – a word that has been used so often and so out of context in the modern media that it has lost its true meaning. A firestorm was a particularly awful phenomenon, in which multiple fires joined together to form one vast city-sized chimney of flame, sucking in air (and people) at hurricane-force speeds for miles around and consuming everything and everyone in it. In the daytime, the towering pillar of flame and smoke would have looked like the atomic clouds above Hiroshima and Nagasaki. It was a unique phenomenon peculiar to huge bombing raids on cities, and it occurred on only a few occasions when an overwhelming avalanche of high-explosive bombs and incendiaries could be delivered to create it. Germany simply did not have the type of heavy bomber aircraft that were needed to deliver these truly massive quantities of bombs.

Had Germany possessed this kind of strategic striking power, however – a power that Wever had always intended it to have – there can be no doubt that Hitler would have used it mercilessly, without hesitation and to maximum effect against the very targets in Britain that *were* indeed bombed. Might we have seen 45,000 dead in Aberdeen? 125,000 dead in Glasgow? The thought of such truly horrific casualty figures taking place in Scotland is a sobering one.

In such an event, might Douhet have been proved right after all? Might the *gallus* Scottish people have been the first to crack and demand an end to the war? We'll never know. As bad as the bombing was, we must be grateful for the intervention of fate in 1936. And that people like Douhet, Wever and Harris have had their day – we hope.

# 1

## *September–December 1939*

### THE NOT-SO-PHONEY WAR

O n a warm and sunny Friday morning on the first day of September 1939, the big Glasgow-registered passenger liner slipped her moorings and headed down the River Clyde, where she had been built. She was a single-funnel steamer weighing over 13,000 tons and was carrying some 1,100 passengers to Montreal in Canada. They crowded the upper decks and admired the scenery as the ship rounded Gourock and turned south down the Firth of Clyde past the white seafront houses and hotels of Dunoon. The distant hills were still draped in the greens of summer and the flat calm waters of the firth reflected the clear blue of the skies above. From Wemyss Bay down to Largs anyone who had cared to glance at this everyday scene of a ship making her majestic way to sea would have witnessed a part of history sailing past them.

The liner was SS *Athenia*, and two days later, on the very day war between Britain and Germany was declared, she would be at the bottom of the Atlantic and 118 of her passengers would be dead, the first British casualties of the Second World War.

*Athenia* was sunk without warning by a U-boat some sixty miles south of Rockall only a matter of hours after a state of war had officially come into place. Having called at Liverpool and Belfast, she set sail for the open Atlantic early on the morning of Sunday, 3 September 1939. Meanwhile, the rest of the British nation famously abandoned their lawn mowers and crowded around their radios to hear Prime Minister Neville Chamberlain make his legendary announcement.

At 11.15 a.m. he broadcast to the nation from the Cabinet Office at 10 Downing Street that a state of war had been declared. Within minutes, a signal had gone out from Berlin ordering all German U-boat commanders at sea to commence hostilities against armed British shipping. Captain James Cook, master of *Athenia*, had also been advised of the outbreak of war and although his ship was an unarmed passenger liner, he ordered the helmsman to start zig-zagging.

This decision sealed the fate of his ship and her passengers.

When Oberleutnant Fritz Lemp, commander of *U-30*, spotted *Athenia* in his periscope, he assumed from the ship's defensive manoeuvres that she must be an armed merchantman and therefore a legitimate target. At 1940 hours (Berlin time) Lemp fired two torpedoes into her side. When *Athenia* immediately issued a distress signal in plain English, Lemp realised his mistake and slunk away, terrified of the wrath of Hitler, who had specifically forbade any civilian casualties for now.

The Donaldson Line's passenger ship had been well built and, thanks also to calm seas and good weather, *Athenia* stayed afloat until the following morning when

SS Athenia *making ready for sea. Torpedoed off Rockall on 3 September 1939 after setting sail from Glasgow, her sinking caused Britain's first civilian casualties of the war.*
(*Courtesy National Archives of Canada*)

three merchant ships and three naval destroyers came to the rescue. There had already been loss of life aboard the ship, thanks to the two huge torpedo explosions, but tragically one of the rescue ships, a Norwegian merchantman named *Knut Neilson*, increased the death toll when it chewed up one of *Athenia's* crowded lifeboats with its propellers. The survivors of the *Athenia* sinking were taken back to the Clyde and landed at Glasgow, where a shocked population waited to meet them. On the first day of the Second World War these first British casualties were all exclusively civilians, many of them children. One of them was only six months old.

It was merely a foretaste of what was to come. By the time the war ended, some 60,000 British civilians would have been killed, and the entire nation would be numbed and hardened to the everyday reality of death and terrible injury. But for now and for the remainder of that year, it was all rather a novelty. In London, newspaper editors wanted war headlines, and the population wanted to read them, yet the Germans did not seem to be delivering the goods. So little seemed to be happening that the phrase 'Phoney War' was conceived to describe the first six months of the war and it has stuck ever since, despite some considerable action in the north. Scotland's coastlines were home to several strategically vital naval bases and anchorages, all of which were perfectly legitimate military targets for German forces. They could be attacked as a show of strength without rocking the boat, which was important because there was a lot more going on behind the scenes than people realised at the time.

Despite the cosy mythology of Britain's resolute defiance of Germany from day one of the war, there is now ample evidence to prove that both sides were working hard to secure a peace before any real fighting broke out between the two countries. Even during October, Hermann Göring was having clandestine face-to-face meetings in Germany with senior British figures, despite the fact that they were at war with each other. Hitler too, had always wanted to avoid war with Britain, and in truth had been shocked when his bluff had been called over Poland, when Britain and France, much to their embarrassment, had been forced to declare war against Germany. Now both Britain and Germany scrabbled to find a solution that would allow both sides to back off from conflict, before things inevitably escalated beyond the point of no return. It was for this reason that Hitler specifically forbade any deaths among the British civilian population – for the moment. As history shows, Hitler had no compunction about killing civilians or anyone else, but as long as there was the slimmest chance of peace with Britain, he was desperate to act the gentleman. Any fighting, he insisted, must be restricted to strictly legitimate naval and military targets. Both sides stuck to this outwardly naïve pattern of behaviour for a while because it suited them. RAF bomber crews, for instance, were warned not to attack any factory buildings in Germany because they were private property.

On the very morning that *Athenia's* passengers were being rescued, the crew of a No. 224 Squadron Coastal Command aircraft at RAF Leuchars in Fife realised that they could now do some shooting of their own. By the time their twin-engine Lockheed Hudson touched down back at Leuchars later that day, they had engaged in the first British air-to-air combat of the war when they attacked a lone German Dornier Do-18 out over the North Sea, though without destroying it. The Hudson's combat was one of many other 'firsts' that would take place in Scotland, thanks to the combination of her strategic location and the offensive restrictions then being imposed by both sides on their military forces. During September, German forces were still heavily engaged in subjugating Poland, and the pace of operations against Britain began to build up quite slowly at first.

*A Lockheed Hudson of the type operating from RAF Leuchars, which engaged a German Dornier Do-18 in the first British air-to-air combat of the war over the North Sea on 4 September 1939. (Courtesy 454 Squadron Association)*

On Friday, 15 September the small 974 ton cargo ship SS *Truro* was making her way from Hull to Norway. As she passed close to Kinnaird Head in Fraserburgh she was attacked by the German submarine *U-36* within sight of shore. After ordering the crew off the ship and into their lifeboats, the U-boat sank *Truro* by gunfire and torpedo. It was all very gentlemanly.

Eleven days later, on the 26 September, it was the turn of the powerful anti-aircraft guns at the huge Royal Navy anchorage at Scapa Flow in Orkney to fire in anger for the first time, followed shortly afterwards by those of the Royal Navy itself. A single Dornier Do-17 P flying from Varel in Germany, droning high over the islands, was hit and damaged by the ferocious barrage of Scapa's defences. The aircraft belonged to the fourth squadron of a dedicated reconnaissance group, Aufklärungsgruppe IV, who would become regular visitors over northern Scotland. On this occasion, the damaged Dornier made it home with only one wounded crew member. But the presence of these aircraft began to spell trouble for the places they had flown over and photographed. A second reconnaissance of Scapa Flow later that day by three Dornier Do-18 flying boats confirmed that the Germans were looking hard for the British Home Fleet, which was at that moment out in the North Sea. When the Dorniers did find the fleet, shortly afterwards, they were given a hot reception. Lieutenant B.S. McEwen, the pilot of an 803 Squadron Fleet Air Arm Blackburn Skua operating from the carrier *Ark Royal*, immediately attacked and shot down Dornier KY+YK. This had the distinction of being the first Luftwaffe aircraft shot down in operations against Great Britain.

But the Dorniers had done their work, reported the position of the fleet back to their base and shortly afterwards nine German Heinkel He-111 and four Junkers Ju-88 bombers arrived to attack it. Already alerted, the FAA Skua fighters were able to beat off the German attack with no conclusive results on either side. But that didn't stop Goebbels' propaganda machine from trying. That night German radio declared that one of the Junkers Ju-88s had sunk the carrier *Ark Royal*. The supposed hero of the hour, a pilot named Unteroffizier Karl Francke, was formally toasted on board *Ark Royal* when the ship's crew heard what he had apparently done to them.

*A Junkers Ju-88 from the bomber wing KG 30, who mounted the first air attack on Britain. This shot shows the confined 'greenhouse' crew arrangement of most German bombers. The diagonal line on the glazing beside the pilot was a guide for dive-bombing – when the line was seen to be parallel with the horizon during a dive, the aircraft was at the correct angle for bomb release. (Courtesy O.I. Vignes)*

During October, a regular pattern began to develop of German reconnaissance and weather flights over Scotland by lone aircraft. Meanwhile, off the Scottish coasts, the U-boats prowled and picked off merchantmen one by one. On 4 October, Otto Kretschmer, captain of *U-23* and a man who would go on to become one of Germany's most famous U-boat commanders, surfaced 60 miles south of Sumburgh Head in Shetland at 6 a.m. He would later develop a taste for laying mines in the Moray Firth, but for now had been trailing the Aberdeen-built SS *Glen Farg* for over an hour, and ordered her to stop with a burst of machine-gun fire into her superstructure. The ship's master, Robert Hall, sailing from Norway back to Aberdeen, tried to get a radio message off but was advised to stop doing so by yet another burst of gunfire, which killed one of Hall's crewmen. Kretschmer ordered Hall to abandon the 876-ton ship then, once the crew were in the lifeboats, sank her with gunfire and a single type G7-A torpedo, before slipping away beneath the waves. (Kretschmer would meet a similar fate (but survive) when sunk in *U-99* in March 1941.) Hall and his crew were picked up by HMS *Firedrake* and landed at Kirkwall the next day.

So far, it was still all very civilised, although it may not have felt quite that way to the German aircrews operating over Scotland. The following day, 5 October, Spitfires of No. 72 Squadron, who had just moved into RAF Drem near Edinburgh, attacked a Heinkel He-111 over the Moray Firth, but only succeeded in damaging it and chasing it off. Three days later, a Dornier Do-18 flying boat from Küstenstaffel 2./KüGr 506 at Hornum See was attacked and shot down by a British aircraft fifteen miles off Aberdeen. The pilot, Leutnant Hornkuhl, was captured. Strangely, no British aircraft claimed the kill, yet if it had been an RAF plane, this would have been the first German aircraft they had shot down. The following day, a Junkers Ju-88 of 1./KG 30 was also shot down with the pilot, Oberleutnant Kahl, and his three fellow crew members all posted as missing in action. Again, no British aircraft claimed the kill. Germany's hunters, on the other hand, were about to prove that they were not so backward at coming forward as the British were.

On 14 October 1939 a particularly daring German U-boat commander named Günther Prien went to Orkney and grabbed the world's headlines in spectacular style. Prien navigated his submerged boat, the *U-47*, through the narrow eastern approaches of Scapa Flow and right into this major British naval anchorage. At precisely 0116 hours he slammed two torpedoes into the side of the mighty battleship *Royal Oak*. The second torpedo blew a 30 foot hole in the side of the First-World-War-era leviathan, which quickly capsized, taking 833 of her 1,400 man crew to the

*The Dornier Do-18 flying boat was a slow and vulnerable aircraft that soon found its position untenable in the skies of eastern Scotland, with several examples being shot down early in the war. This machine is shown being attacked after being forced down by a 220 Squadron Lockheed Hudson from RAF Wick. (Courtesy F.E. Clarke Collection)*

bottom with her, while Prien and his crew made their escape. In London the First Sea Lord, Winston Churchill, currently in charge of the admiralty and stung by the storm of protest over the sinking, ordered the construction of the barriers that now bear his name between the Orkney mainland and the islands of Burray and South Ronaldsay, and also ordered no less than four squadrons of fighters to be based at Wick. This was a classic case of shutting the stable door after the horse has bolted, and an absolute triumph of propaganda for the German Kriegsmarine. Only one man in all of Germany was anything less than ecstatic about the sinking – Hermann Göring.

The intense rivalry between his commanders, which Hitler actively encouraged, was one of the great motivating factors (but also one of the great weaknesses) of the German armed forces. Each wanted to impress Hitler most in order to secure further power, prestige and resources for his particular command. Göring now needed and demanded an equally spectacular success story from his Luftwaffe. Two days later his crews tried but failed to deliver it to him. It would not be the last time that Hitler would be given cause to lose faith in Göring and his incorrectly equipped Luftwaffe. Nonetheless the raid was on, and the target once again was a major British capital ship. Göring's reconnaissance planes had been over Scotland again and had plotted the location of the mighty battleship HMS *Hood* in dock at Rosyth. Sinking this ship, the pride of the Royal Navy, would easily rival Prien's success at Scapa Flow, provided, of course, the German planes could get through to the target and home again. The problem was that the Firth of Forth was a long way from the nearest available German airfield at Westerland on the Island of Sylt near the Danish border. Over a round-trip distance of more than 1,000 miles, no Luftwaffe fighter could accompany the bombers all the way there and back. Apart from the anti-aircraft defences around Rosyth, which were sure to be on alert after the disaster at Scapa, the Forth area was well protected by fighter airfields at Turnhouse and Drem, where two squadrons of local auxiliary air force 'weekend flyers', numbers 602 and 603, were not only waiting for action but also very highly motivated to prove themselves.

The crews of No. 1 section of bomber squadron Kampfgeschwader 30 (1./KG 30) were briefed for the mission and told the facts, yet still did not think the mission was in any way as dangerous as later German crews attacking the Forth would consider this target (one later named 'Suicide Alley') to be. For one thing, they were equipped with the brand-new Junkers Ju-88 A-1 bomber, an aircraft specifically designed as the *Schnellbomber* (literally 'fast bomber'). It was intended, rather naïvely, to be able to outrun single-engine fighters like the Spitfire. Unfortunately for the German crews the chief of the Luftwaffe's technical inspectorate was an old-school pilot and friend of Göring's named Ernst Udet, who was woefully incapable of doing his job but who had fallen in love with the concept of dive-bombers like the Junkers Ju-87 Stuka. Consequently, he had made the incredible decision of ordering *all* German bombers to be capable of dive-bombing. It was yet another crazy decision that the Luftwaffe found itself shackled with. The extra weight of dive brakes and other equipment required to allow the Junkers Ju-88 to perform as a dive-bomber, turned the new *Schnellbomber* into a pitifully slow bomber when it came to mixing with Spitfires, as the crews were about to find out. At noon the raid leader, Hauptmann Helmut Pohle, led his formation of twelve aircraft into the air from Sylt. One of the bombers immediately crashed on take-off. The rest set course for Scotland, hoping that this was not a bad omen and that Lady Luck would be on their side. As it turned out, she already was.

Much has been written about this first German attack on the British mainland, which took everyone completely by surprise, and even to this day questions are still being asked and accusations made about what went wrong on the British side. No air-raid warning was sounded, no anti-aircraft batteries were ready, no fighters were scrambled and a train was actually passing over the Forth Bridge as the German formation began its attack. The anti-aircraft defences in particular were roundly but unjustly condemned by their own boss, Sir Frederick Pile, when in reality he should have been complimenting them on the speed of their reaction despite no warning having been given. Such a fuss was made about it all in the press that Prime Minister Neville Chamberlain felt compelled to lie to the House of Commons, when he explained that a conscious decision was made that it was 'not appropriate' to raise the alarm, because this would have caused 'dislocation and inconvenience over a wide area'. The truth of the matter was that no warning *could* be given to any of the defences around Edinburgh or even to the civilian population, simply because the British early-warning radar system had failed to detect the incoming raid. In fact it had not been capable of detecting anything that day, because it wasn't working.

It has only recently been revealed that the Chain Home radar site at Drone Hill, which provided long-range early-warning for the Firth of Forth approaches and for

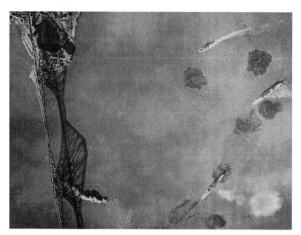

*A German photograph of the attack on Royal Navy warships in the Firth of Forth on 16 October 1939, taken while the attack was still in progress. The dark circles near the ships indicate where mud from the bed of the Forth has been churned up by bomb explosions. (Courtesy University of Wellington, New Zealand)*

the greater Edinburgh area, went out of service that very morning due to a blown valve and could not be repaired until the following day. Suspicious minds might have detected a conspiracy, but it was nothing more than a pure fluke and 1./KG 30 were to benefit from it, if only in terms of survival.

At around 2.00 p.m. on 16 October the undetected German force arrived over 'Walrus' (the German codename for Rosyth) looking for *Hood*. But the ship the reconnaissance planes had spotted was not *Hood* but the battleship *Repulse* and since she was in dock, she could not be attacked for fear of killing civilians nearby – an action which seems astounding when one considers the devastation that bombers of all sides would be happy to wreak on ports and harbours later in the war. Instead Pohle's formation selected alternative targets: two fat warships anchored off Inchgarvie, 500 yards east of the Forth Bridge. As the bombers were diving to attack the cruisers HMS *Edinburgh* and HMS *Southampton,* the sound of their engines alerted everyone in the area and despite the unfair criticisms of defences being taken by surprise, all of them leapt into action with commendable speed under the circumstances. Anti-aircraft guns started blazing away, barking so loudly that they could be heard in central Edinburgh, while the scramble order was given to the eagerly waiting Spitfire crews at Turnhouse and Drem. Meanwhile, Pohle and his crews had dropped their 500 kg bombs and were already starting to turn for home in a classic example of a hit-and-run raid. Both cruisers were hit. One bomb went right through *Southampton* and out the bottom before exploding, wrecking an admiral's barge and a pinnace. There were surprisingly few casualties on the ships, with only some ten injuries in all, although some sixteen men were killed half an hour after the main raid aboard the destroyer HMS *Mohawk,* when it was attacked out in the estuary by the last remnants of the attacking force.

Now it was time to run, but the speed of reaction of the Spitfire crews was quite superb and already they were in the air and hunting for targets. It soon became clear that the German *Schnellbombers* could not 'schnell' away from trouble as quickly as had been claimed. There has always been some debate about which British pilot was first to shoot down one of the two Ju-88s that were destroyed that day, but contemporary historians say that Flight Lieutenant Patrick 'Patsy' Gifford of 603 Squadron shot down aircraft 4D+DH piloted by Leutnant Storp four miles off Port Seton at 1445 hours, while Flight Lieutenant George Pinkerton in a Spitfire of 602 Squadron shot down the German strike leader himself, Helmut Pohle, ten minutes later. This aircraft crashed into the sea three miles east of Crail at 1455 hours. A third German aircraft, flown by Leutnant von Riesen, was badly damaged by Spitfires but made it back to Westerland.

This was the first time the Luftwaffe encountered the Spitfire in battle, a full eight months before (as is often claimed) they were supposedly 'shocked' to meet Spitfires for the first time over Dunkirk.

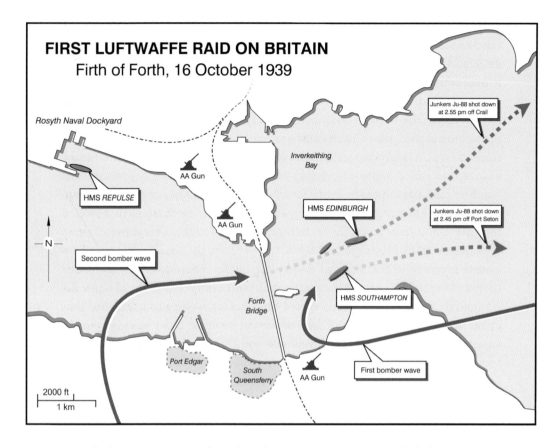

**FIRST LUFTWAFFE RAID ON BRITAIN**
Firth of Forth, 16 October 1939

Rosyth Naval Dockyard

Inverkeithing Bay

Junkers Ju-88 shot down at 2.55 pm off Crail

AA Gun

HMS *REPULSE*

HMS *EDINBURGH*

AA Gun

Junkers Ju-88 shot down at 2.45 pm off Port Seton

— N —

Second bomber wave

HMS *SOUTHAMPTON*

Forth Bridge

Port Edgar

South Queensferry

AA Gun

First bomber wave

2000 ft

1 km

The last German aircraft to clear the target area were harried all the way out to sea by Spitfires from 603 Squadron, two of which chased a single Ju-88 at rooftop height right across Edinburgh, firing at it all the way. For the people below this was not much fun. The Spitfires were equipped with eight Browning rifle-calibre machine guns, which sprayed bullets outwards in cones of fire in order to hit their targets. These cones of fire now lashed out across the streets of Edinburgh and Portobello, causing the first civilian casualty on mainland Britain. Joe McLuskie was a painter and decorator giving some windows a lick of paint on a house in Portobello when he was hit in the stomach by a bullet and had to have an emergency operation to remove it, as did John Ferry at West Pilton, who was hit in the leg. In both cases, their non-fatal injuries were caused by bullets from 603 Squadron's Spitfires, as was considerable minor damage all over the city, including at the Lord Provost's house, although in all cases the Spitfire pilots were graciously forgiven.

Much was subsequently written in the British press and in books about this symbolic and exciting first German air attack on mainland Britain and much is still being written, some of it untrue. In a recent newspaper article headed *The Scot who bombed his homeland for the Nazis* (with the word 'Nazis' printed in bold red ink), it was claimed that one of the German pilots who attacked the Forth that day was one Frederick Hansen, a born-and-bred Scot from Melrose in the Borders who had emigrated to Germany with his German father and Scottish mother before the war began. In dramatic terms, the article explained how Hansen returned to attack his home country of Scotland, but how he had paid with his life when he was killed in the attack that day. It would have been a great story had it been true. Hansen was not killed that day because he did not even take part in the raid, as the attack leader Helmut Pohle himself has confirmed. Hansen was killed in Holland in 1941 and besides, he was a radio operator, not a pilot.

For the surviving crews of KG 30 at Westerland, there was a surprise in store for them back at base. They were going back to Scotland again the next day, this time to Scapa Flow, a location already as dangerous to their health as Rosyth was starting to become. On 17 October, as Britain was digesting the newspaper headlines of the Forth raid over their morning toast, four Junkers Ju-88s attacked Scapa, looking once more in vain for the British Home Fleet, which had not returned to Orkney since the *Royal Oak* sinking three days before. What the raiders found instead was the tired old First World War battleship HMS *Iron Duke*, which was now seeing out her last days as a depot ship. The Ju-88s dived down from 11,000 feet and released their bombs from 700 feet, scoring two direct hits on the old ship which immediately began to sink. Luckily, a tug managed to get a line aboard the battleship and towed her to Ore Bay where she was successfully beached. On board *Iron Duke*, one man was killed and twenty-five injured.

Meanwhile, the shore batteries had already started to let fly at the German raiders. On the little island of Rysa at Hoy, No. 1 gun of 226 Heavy Anti-Aircraft battery (HAA) blew the glazed nose clean off a raider with a four-and-a-half-inch anti-aircraft shell. The nose landed right beside the gun crew while the German aircraft plummeted straight down in flames and crashed at the mouth of Pegal Burn on Hoy. Amazingly, Fritz Ambrosius, the German radio operator, parachuted out at low level and despite suffering severe burns survived to be captured. His captain, Oberleutnant Flaemig and another crew member were killed in this, the first German aircraft to be shot down on British soil.

At least the newspapers were getting something to write about during the 'Phoney War'.

On 21 October a Heinkel He-115 B floatplane strayed too close to the Scottish coast near Aberdeen and was shot down into the sea by a British fighter. Oberleutnant Peinemann and his crew from the first wing of Küstenstaffelgruppe 406 (Coastal Squadron Group) were killed. Further south a week later came the celebrated downing of a Heinkel He-111. This was not because it was the first shot down on British soil (as was incorrectly claimed), but because it was the first that people could actually go along and *see*. Flown by Unteroffizier Kurt Lehmkuhl of

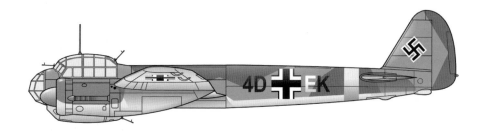

## FIRST GERMAN AIRCRAFT SHOT DOWN ON BRITISH SOIL

Junkers Ju-88 A-1 of *Kampfgeschwader* 30
Shot down by 226 Heavy Anti-Aircraft Battery
at Hoy, Orkney Islands, on 17 October 1939

KG 26, based at Westerland, the Heinkel was attacked by Spitfires of 602 and 603 Squadrons and forced down at Newton Farm, Humbie, south of Edinburgh. In truth, however, the aircraft had already been mortally wounded by anti-aircraft fire from a number of naval ships off the Forth estuary, one of which, HMS *Mohawk*, had good reason to be trigger-happy against German aircraft. The pilot, although wounded, had successfully brought the aircraft down in one piece on very difficult terrain. The wreck itself quickly became a world-wide celebrity and the aircraft was estimated to have attracted literally thousands of visitors before it was eventually removed from the scene, with sightseers and photographers travelling from as far away as London to see this unique enemy aircraft specimen.

Soon they would all have plenty of wrecked aircraft to look at closer to home.

The month of October ended with the sinking of another cargo ship close to the Scottish east coast. The SS *Cairnmona* was a large 4,666 ton cargo ship on her way from Montreal to the Tyne. Three miles off Rattray Head the German submarine *U-13* spotted her and torpedoed her, this time, apparently without warning. The ship was quickly ablaze and three firemen died when the ship rolled over and sank. Forty-two survivors were picked up by the passing Aberdeen trawler *River Lossie*. It was beginning to look as if the brief age of chivalry among the U-boat captains was coming to an end.

The rest of the year would be dominated by air activity, and 13 November 1939 saw the small village of Sullom Voe in Shetland suffer what was (technically, at least) the first German bomb to land on British soil. Had this relatively unknown place been elevated at that time to its modern-day status as one of the biggest oil-tanker loading terminals in Europe, the results of that single bomb-drop might have had far more serious implications than the reputed demise of a rabbit that was killed. This rabbit well illustrates how speculation can turn into legend. It is repeatedly claimed

*The famous 'Humbie Heinkel' from KG 26, which was shot down by Spitfires from 602 and 603 Squadrons and which force-landed at Newton Farm, Humbie, in October 1939. For a while, it became the most photographed aircraft in the world, when the idea of being at war was still something of a novelty. (Courtesy Museum of Flight)*

that this sole casualty of the bomb inspired the popular wartime song *Run Rabbit Run*. Despite the fact that the song is all about a shotgun-armed farmer who was apparently fond of rabbit pie and nothing to do with German bombs, it's a safe bet to assume that the writers of the song, Flanagan and Allen, would never have heard of Sullom Voe in the first place.

On 22 November an RAF Saro London flying boat of 210 Squadron was moored in Lerwick's north harbour having an engine changed, when six Heinkel He-111 bombers appeared over Lerwick and began circling the town looking for targets. They soon settled on the flying boat and one after another tried to hit her. After eight bombs had been dropped to no effect, one clearly frustrated German pilot swooped in low and strafed the British seaplane with machine-gun fire, setting it alight. Satisfied, the German bombers set off for the long haul back to Germany, while the six men working on the flying boat were picked up by the harbour lifeboat.

This seemed to be a lot of effort for a fairly marginal result in these increasingly dangerous British skies. Yet some German bombers seemed to lead charmed lives. The following day, a lone Heinkel He-111 from the reconnaissance unit 1(F)./122 flew right over every major naval base in Scotland, snapping away with its cameras without being intercepted. It appeared over the Clyde, then flew to Rosyth to take a look, turned north and droned on over Dundee, Aberdeen, the Moray Firth and once around Invergordon before heading north to Scapa Flow, where it was finally fired at by a patrolling British fighter. Even then the Heinkel still got away, crash-landing at Borkum Island in Germany. So much for modern integrated air defences.

Two weeks later, this recce unit would not be so lucky. Although three aircraft set out for the distant Moray Firth on 6 December 1939, only one of them made it that far after two of the Heinkels crashed on take-off. The third was shot down over the Moray Firth, with one of the crew being killed. The next day, two more Heinkels went down into the sea off the Scottish coast. The bomber wing KG 26 had attacked a convoy off the mouth of the River Tay but were then immediately attacked themselves and driven off by Spitfires from numbers 603 and 72 Squadrons at Drem. The German crews all died. Less than two weeks later, a Saro London flying boat from 240 Squadron at Sullom Voe extracted a little revenge for the Lerwick harbour incident (and perhaps also for the rabbit) when it attacked and damaged a Heinkel He-111 of KG 26 over the North Sea. The Heinkel limped back to Westerland, where it was found to be so badly damaged by the crash-landing that it was written off, the only 'kill' ever achieved by a Saro London.

Three days later, on 21 December, disaster struck the two Spitfire squadrons from Drem, when 602 and 72 squadrons aircraft attacked a pair of twin-engine bombers over the Firth of Forth and shot them both down. The bombers, unfortunately, were British Handley Page Hampdens from 44 Squadron en route from Waddington to Leuchars. Sixty years before the phrase 'friendly fire' was invented, a crewman of 44 Squadron was killed by this tragically all-too-common wartime phenomenon. The Drem Spitfires acquitted themselves the very next day, however, when a section from 602 Squadron intercepted a Heinkel He-111 of KG 26 and a Ju-88 over the Isle of May and shot down the Heinkel. The Junkers made it back to base but never flew again: so ended the first four months of war in Scotland.

The pace had been busy but not hectic. Casualties had still been mercifully light all round. And so far neither Britain nor Germany had tried out General Douhet's theories on each other.

But the war was still young.

# 2

## *1939–1945*

## THE AIR DEFENCE OF SCOTLAND

Air Vice-Marshal Sir Hugh Dowding, head of RAF Fighter Command during the Battle of Britain, has recently been described on the cover of a book as 'One of History's Greatest Englishmen'.

He was born at Moffat in Dumfriesshire in April 1882 and went to the local St Ninian's Boys Preparatory School, before starting a traditional military career in the south by attending Winchester College and the Royal Military Academy. The compliment of being elevated to something beyond a mere Scotsman, therefore, is perhaps doubly justified, because if one man can be said to have won the Battle of Britain, it is Hugh Dowding. He is now considered to be as important a figure in British history as Sir Francis Drake or Admiral Lord Nelson. Clearly though, this was not always the case and any casual glance at Trafalgar Square will confirm that there is no 'Dowding's Column' alongside Nelson's. The story of the wartime plot against Dowding is a book in itself, however; suffice to say that the importance of the man and his contribution to British history is now at last being widely recognised.

Dowding's tactics for the air defence of the British Isles are now universally acknowledged as quite simply the only ones that could possibly have worked. These tactics were to use his fighters sparingly, never commit them all at once, and thereby always have fighters available to deal with other raids that radar detected coming in from other locations. It preserved Dowding's fighter force, and meant that nearly

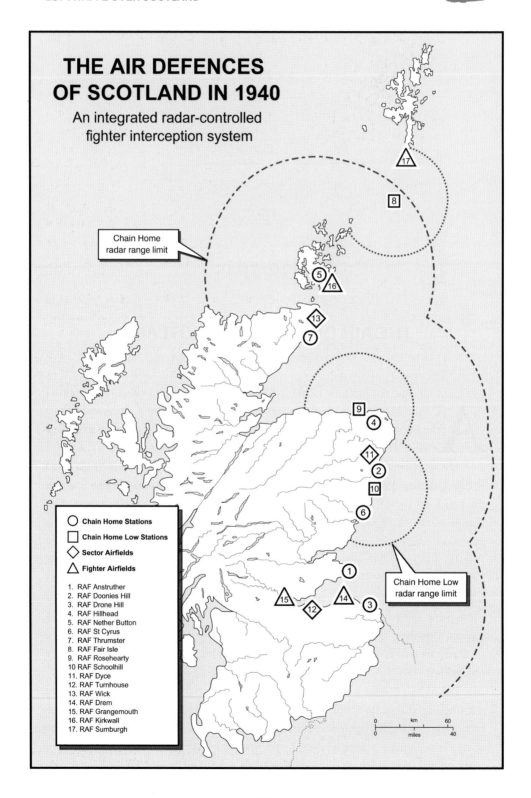

**THE AIR DEFENCES OF SCOTLAND IN 1940**

An integrated radar-controlled fighter interception system

Chain Home radar range limit

Chain Home Low radar range limit

○ Chain Home Stations
□ Chain Home Low Stations
◇ Sector Airfields
△ Fighter Airfields

1. RAF Anstruther
2. RAF Doonies Hill
3. RAF Drone Hill
4. RAF Hillhead
5. RAF Nether Button
6. RAF St Cyrus
7. RAF Thrumster
8. RAF Fair Isle
9. RAF Rosehearty
10 RAF Schoolhill
11. RAF Dyce
12. RAF Turnhouse
13. RAF Wick
14. RAF Drem
15. RAF Grangemouth
16. RAF Kirkwall
17. RAF Sumburgh

km   miles

every incoming German raid could be met by fighter opposition: simple but brilliant. And it worked.

An alternative tactic involving the use of the so-called 'Big Wing' theory needs to be highlighted in any consideration of the Battle of Britain. The Big Wing tactics were the complete opposite to Dowding's and involved forming-up huge formations of fighters then sending them off to look for enemy aircraft, rather than reacting to incoming raids that were detected by radar. This was a tactic the Germans hoped would be used by the British, but one they themselves were never foolish enough to employ when forced to defend their own skies against incoming Allied bombers. The Big Wing's greatest flaw (and it had many) was that the entire force could be easily fooled by one or more spoof raids, allowing other raids to sneak in unopposed and do their damage. If the damage in question had happened to be to the Big Wings themselves refuelling on the ground back at base, Britain would very quickly have run out of fighters and pilots.

Radar, as most people know, was the key to the successful defence of Britain in the Second World War. Or to put it more accurately, the key was how the information radar provided was *used*.

The British radar system (Germany had radar by then as well) was known as RDF, for Radio Direction Finding, and consisted of a series of stations built at key points in a chain all along the south and east coasts of Britain, since it was always assumed that this was the direction any threat would come from. Consequently, it was called the Chain Home (CH) system. Some of these sites still survive today, particularly the one at Hillhead in deepest Aberdeenshire, which must be one of the most untouched and original wartime military installations in the country. In each of these sites, the core of the complex is two brick buildings shrouded by massive

*A typical Chain Home radar station during the Second World War. The four masts in the foreground are the transmitting masts, while the four receiving masts are in the background. Despite their fragile appearance, these masts were very strong and their open lattice construction absorbed bomb explosions well. (Courtesy Bawdsey Radar Association)*

concrete external walls and 6-foot-thick concrete roofs, all designed to survive the blast of a 1,000 lb bomb (and in the case of Hillhead, more than sixty years of harsh Scottish winters as well). Giant masts announced the location of these strategic sites to anyone with a pair of eyes. All the stations overlapped and stretched from Bristol to Shetland. They could detect incoming aircraft flying in at great height and at considerable distances away. At each station one of the concrete bunkers contained a transmitting room, which sent out the required radio pulses, and the other contained a receiving room, which dealt with any pulses that were bounced straight back from objects in the sky. Using these returned signals WAAF operators identified the existence of distant aircraft approaching the coastlines by means of vertical lines (or 'blips') shown on their primitive cathode ray tubes. Once plotted, the information providing height, course, speed and bearing of each incoming raid (a raid being anything from a single aircraft to a massed formation) was immediately passed along to the headquarters of No. 13 Group in Newcastle, who were responsible for all of the airspace in Scotland.

The information received at Group HQ was passed to one of the three sector operations rooms in Scotland, which were at the RAF airfields at Wick, Turnhouse and Dyce. Here raids were plotted using a simple graphical system on a table showing a map of the entire area. WAAFs, in direct radio contact with the radar stations and airfields, moved numbered symbols around the board to represent aircraft dispositions in almost 'real time'. The beauty of this system was that the controllers up on a balcony above the table could tell at a single glance the current position of all their own aircraft and all the hostile ones, and order the required fighters to the right area for an interception. But Scotland had a huge amount of airspace and few fighters to cover it all with, so care was needed. In addition to the sector airfields, Scotland had only four dedicated fighter airfields at Drem, Grangemouth, Kirkwall and Sumburgh.

*Pilots and ground crew pose beside a Supermarine Spitfire of the type that equipped many of the squadrons defending Scotland's airspace, primarily 602 (City of Glasgow) and 603 (City of Edinburgh) Squadrons. (Courtesy US National Archives)*

*Hawker Hurricane fighter of the type that equipped many squadrons in Scotland during the first few years of the war, including units such as 43 Squadron, who were based at Wick at the time of the Orkney battles. (Courtesy RAF Museum)*

At these sector airfields the pilots were not allowed to go off on solo hunting expeditions, but were strictly controlled and kept waiting until needed. Even when an incoming raid was detected, a good controller would try to get a feel for the direction and strength of the incoming raid before deciding which fighter units – and how many of them – to send off to intercept the bandits. By keeping most of his available fighters still waiting on the ground, a controller could instantly allocate other fighters to deal with a new threat from a different direction and in a different area. Pilots were kept waiting at a state of readiness, their aircraft fully fuelled and fully armed, their engines constantly warmed up and a mechanic with a trolley accumulator plugged into the aircraft, ready to fire everything up as soon as the controller phoned the dispersal ready room and the order was shouted, 'Scramble, red section!' Only after they were airborne as fast as possible (which was the first priority) would the fighter pilots be directed precisely to their designated target area, where they had a high chance of intercepting the detected hostile aircraft.

It was a good system and it usually worked, provided the radar stations did not go offline, as happened at Drone Hill that day on 16 October 1939. Unfortunately, however, there was another problem with the radar system that soon became obvious. Chain Home radar had a fatal weakness – it could not detect anything flying below 3,000 feet, at least not until the aircraft in question was almost on top of it. To deal with this problem of enemy aircraft being able to fly in under the radar, an additional system was introduced that became much more important as far as Scotland was concerned, because raids always came in at low level to give almost no possibility of warning to coastal targets. The Chain Home Low system (CHL) was brought in to catch aircraft flying at these lower levels, but even then there was still a considerable gap below which CHL could not see, and German aircraft continued to exploit this by coming in at extremely low level (100 feet was the norm) and were still catching the defences by surprise. To make matters worse, because the radar stations all pointed out to sea, once German bombers had crossed the British coasts, radar could no longer detect them. This is where the Observer Corps came into play.

It would seem an anachronism for a complex modern defence system to have to revert to the Mark I human eyeball, but it actually worked, and worked very well.

Whereas most people would simply look up to see only an anonymous aeroplane droning across the sky, members of the Observer Corps were able (mostly through self-training) to recognise the shape of literally any type of contemporary aircraft and correctly identify it at any height or distance. Even as recently as the 1970s, this writer took part in an aircraft recognition contest as an air cadet (teenagers did not have so many leisure-time options in those days), in which photographs showing impossibly small images of aircraft were flashed up on screen for less than a second, one after the other, for perhaps twenty or thirty aircraft. The participants were required to write down the *exact* type of aircraft (and sometimes even the make of the aircraft as well) on a competition form. What was most staggering of all was that the Observer Corps people almost always achieved a one hundred per cent success rate. It was a matter of pride, and it was a very valuable skill in wartime. If an enemy aircraft was spotted by a member of the Observer Corps, the controller receiving the telephoned information about aircraft type, height, heading, bearing and distance would always be able to trust the information completely.

*A battery of searchlights in operation during the Second World War gives an idea of the power and range of these lights, designed to trap an aircraft in a cone of light for anti-aircraft gunners to engage. (Courtesy Skylighters Association)*

But even the Observer Corps couldn't see in the dark. When all else failed, searchlights and anti-aircraft guns were the last resort. Britain's anti-aircraft guns were divided into two separate categories, the Heavy Anti-Aircraft batteries (HAA) and Light Anti-Aircraft batteries (LAA). The HAA guns were usually in the 3 inch to 4.5 inch calibre range, although heavier guns were also used. Unlike the outstanding German 88 mm *Flak* gun, which was fully mobile and could be quickly set up pretty much anywhere, British HAA guns required permanent infrastructures built for them in the form of concrete bases and support buildings. These were dotted all around the country at strategic locations, such as at the big ICI explosives works at Ardeer in Ayrshire, and many survive in overgrown locations to this day.

It is worth noting that long-range HAA guns did not rely on scoring a direct hit on an enemy aircraft to bring it down, which was very nearly impossible against high-flying aircraft anyway. Instead the HAA guns relied on a proximity explosion in order to destroy or wound an enemy bomber. Once the height of an incoming raid had been decided, a member of each gun crew would turn a knurled dial on the nose cone of each shell to a height setting at which the shell would then be fused to

*A preserved British 3.7 inch HAA gun. These guns were generally located at fixed emplacements, requiring considerable built infrastructure such as the mountings shown here. The shells fired were normally proximity fused, designed to shower shrapnel around the sky near their intended target. (Author's collection)*

explode. High up in the sky, even if the shell exploded as much as 1,000 feet short of an enemy aircraft, there was a reasonable chance that the hundreds of red-hot fragments of shrapnel, designed to lash out in every direction, would pierce a vital part of a bomber and either set it on fire or blow it up. It worked surprisingly often, and yet it is claimed that the main purpose of having anti-aircraft guns sited around towns and cities in the Second World War (on both sides) was to reassure the public at large that they were being protected from air raids as well as possible. It is a well-recorded fact that the incredible racket of massed anti-aircraft artillery firing over a city would often, to paraphrase Wellington, scare the hell out of the public more than it did the enemy.

The LAA artillery were mostly 40 mm Bofors guns, which were mobile weapons that could be sited anywhere and required only a sandbagged wall built around them to give some protection for the crews. These guns were designed for use against low-flying aircraft and were therefore particularly valuable in Scotland, where most raids, with the notable exception of Clydebank and Greenock, came in at very low level. The legend of Aberdeen's 'Bofors Spy' is worth recounting, if only to demonstrate the fact that these guns were so widely used in Scotland. Several batteries of these

*The crew of a 40 mm Bofors LAA gun somewhere in Scotland during the Second World War. These were excellent short-range weapons and, in contrast to the proximity-fused HAA guns, fired 'hit or miss' ammunition directly against low-flying enemy aircraft, and were much more effective in this role than is widely recognised. One hit was usually enough to bring down an enemy aircraft. (Author's collection)*

guns were sited all along the long Beach Boulevard in Aberdeen in a perfect location to engage enemy raiders coming in from the sea. When each raid subsequently came into Aberdeen from every direction *but* from the sea, it was rumoured that a local spy had told the Germans that these batteries were sited here and so the bombers avoided them. The day after the Bofors guns were relocated elsewhere in Aberdeen, a raider came straight in from the sea at low-level over the Beach Boulevard and attacked Aberdeen without a shot being fired at it. The next day the Bofors guns were once again set up all along the Beach Boulevard and the German bombers never came straight in over the Boulevard again. So the legend says, anyway.

*This Junkers Ju-88 of KG 30 in Norway was hit by ground fire from a low-level mission over Scotland, and returned to base bearing the scars. The bullet holes seem to be of rifle calibre, so it is likely that the aircraft was shot at by a machine-gunner on ship or shore as it passed over its target at low level and high speed.*
*(Courtesy O.I. Vignes)*

When every defensive measure had been exhausted and the bombs started falling, the very last resort for the civilian population was to find somewhere to hide – quickly. This was all very well when a siren was sounded to provide the 'Red' air-raid warning signal, meaning an attack was imminent, but because of the inability to detect low-level coastal raiders until they were overhead, sirens often sounded in towns like Fraserburgh long *after* the bombers had been and gone, but usually they never sounded at all, because the deed was done and the skies were once again all clear.

There can be few things as terrifying as being bombed at random in your own home surroundings, with little or no warning about what is going to happen. In most Scottish towns, small poured-concrete air-raid shelters were thrown up all over the place, with very few actually being sited underground. None could withstand a direct hit, of course, but it was the legal duty of the civil defence authorities to provide *something*, and quite often these shelters were just enough to prevent death or injury from blast and shrapnel from a bomb exploding nearby. Civil defence authorities

*An army bomb-disposal team unearths an unexploded German 1,000 kg bomb prior to defusing it. On both sides during the war an enormous amount of bombs failed to explode, although it became standard practice for the RAF to drop bombs with long-delay fuses. These were designed to look like unexploded bombs, which would then explode while specially trained bomb-disposal experts were digging them out.*
*(Courtesy* Illustrated *magazine)*

were also responsible for ensuring that all populated areas had sufficient first-aid posts in place to deal with casualties, as well as rest centres to temporarily house people who had lost their homes. And there were plenty of them. In the aftermath of the Clydebank raids of March 1941, a staggering 55,000 people required rehousing. As always, people in every nation afflicted by wartime bombing rallied round and helped each other out. All of Britain was full of evacuated children or bombed-out families who suddenly found themselves living with total strangers. There was an air of everyone being in it together. But of course, not everyone was happy about it.

Glasgow City archives contain a letter from a furious shopkeeper in Rothesay who demanded at great length that the filthy, undisciplined children from Glasgow who had been moved into the area be immediately moved out again, and to hell with the bombing. He stated that the local constabulary were in a position to confirm that one of these children had actually stolen a chocolate bar from his shop.

Many people, of course, were not lucky enough to be simply bombed out of their houses and were instead killed inside them. Rescue teams would search for days without rest until as many bodies as possible had been recovered. But there were also survivors to dig out. The old cliché of hiding in the cupboard under the stairs was not as naïve as it sounds. A staircase is a very strong structure, and their angled shape could often deflect tons of masonry and rubble that collapsed down upon them, leaving survivors trapped deep inside a huge pile of rubble that had to be cleared away by hand.

Larger German bombs in the 1,000 kg category could kill by concussion alone, or cause a victim to be shredded to death simply by flying glass, while incendiaries could start fires inside buildings that had been opened up by the blast effect of such

*The scene at Baxter Street in Greenock, clearly showing the wider effects of bomb blasts. Although no building has been directly hit by a bomb, a nearby blast has blown off roofs, doors, windows and even part of some of the frontages of all the houses in the picture. This was the 'dehousing' effect of air raids. (Courtesy Speirs family archive)*

a bomb. But that's not all a near miss could do. Bombs exploding anywhere near buildings and houses always had side-effects other than killing people.

A photographer in Greenock took one particularly interesting photograph in Baxter Street in the aftermath of the 1941 raids. In this so typically Scottish street, a bomb has clearly fallen somewhere nearby and although no single house has been directly hit, blast damage is extensive. Almost every single window and every single door of every single house has been blasted clean away, leaving only shells.

The effect on the people who lived there must have been terrible. Having escaped death or injury, an enormous number of Scots still found themselves facing an identical scene to this one in the aftermath of a bombing raid. They had been 'dehoused' as the term put it, and must have been deeply distressed.

But then again, that was precisely what General Douhet had been hoping for.

# 3

## *1940*

## SCOTLAND'S LONGEST YEAR

The common perception of the year 1940 is one of great air battles high over the white cliffs of Dover during a long hot summer. Naturally, this is only part of the story, but as we shall see, that story involves Scotland considerably more than is widely recognised.

For instance, traditional versions of the Battle of Britain assure us that the German Luftwaffe encountered the radar-directed fighter interception system of the RAF for the first time over the English Channel that summer, and for the first time suffered heavy losses as a result. It may therefore come as a surprise to discover that in reality the Luftwaffe first encountered Britain's new radar-based air defences in the skies over Orkney and the Pentland Firth in April, and that in so doing they suffered their first heavy losses in great air battles over northern Scotland, long before the Battle of Britain officially began in July.

On New Year's Day itself, British and German aircraft resumed hostilities over Scotland when an obsolete Gloster Gladiator biplane fighter (all that the RAF would spare) of the Shetland Fighter Force took on and shot down the first of ten German raiders destroyed over Scotland before the end of March alone. The pace never slackened in the north from then onwards.

Those first few days of 1940 saw ships in Scottish waters being sunk without warning. On 3 January SS *Svarton* went down off Fraserburgh with 20 crewmen killed, while SS *Gowrie* was sunk off Stonehaven by German bombers five days later.

A particular tragedy occurred on 21 January, when the destroyer HMS *Exmouth* was torpedoed off Wick by the German submarine *U-22*. The warship immediately exploded, broke in half and went down with all 189 officers and men aboard her. The bodies of the crew were washed ashore all the way up the coast from Brora to Wick in the following days and weeks. Clearly 1940 was going to be a long year of war in Scotland.

As if in retribution for the spate of New Year sinkings, Spitfires and Hurricanes from fighter squadrons based at airfields around northern Scotland began taking a steady toll of German bombers off the Scottish coasts. Yet no matter whether they were friend or foe, the heartless North Sea always took her time to give up her casualties of war. The bodies of one Heinkel bomber crew were washed up at Rattray Head a full two weeks after a Spitfire of 603 Squadron had shot it down off Aberdeen on 19 January.

RAF fighters were making life very hard for the German bombers, but in the huge airspace of Scotland their relatively small numbers meant they could not be everywhere at once. None could help on 30 January, when the Leith-registered cargo ship SS *Giralda* was sunk by Heinkels of KG 26 off South Ronaldsay in Orkney. The locals who gathered on the beach to try to help could only watch in horror as 23 survivors from the ship died when their lifeboat capsized in rough seas offshore. Dealing with the ferocity of a typical Scottish winter was bad enough without having to fight a war into the bargain.

A good example of this harsh fact took place the following night at the height of that terrible gale. The 2,297 ton Swedish cargo ship SS *Fram* was sheltering in Aberdour Bay when she was torpedoed a mile from shore by *U-13* and blown clean in half. Twenty died, while five survivors were miraculously saved from the sea and taken to Macduff by a local fishing boat. Because of the howling storm carrying all sounds out to sea, the huddled residents in the cliff-top village of New Aberdour heard nothing of the explosion nor saw anything of the tragedy.

In the skies above, the fighting went on. A typical action in February saw a single Ju-88 attacking a Royal Navy minesweeper in the Moray Firth and being blown out of the sky by the ship's anti-aircraft gunners for its troubles, the surviving crew being fished out of the water by the gleeful sailors. The national press continued to be fed news from Scotland, with one particularly welcome Heinkel being delivered for national consumption courtesy of 602 Squadron's Spitfires. The wounded German pilot brought the machine down near North Berwick Law, where it clipped a hedge and tipped up on its nose in a highly photogenic pose for the benefit of the cameras. Almost undamaged, the aircraft was soon back in the air, wearing British markings, for evaluation purposes. Both sides loved to play with aircraft captured from their opponents, and captured Spitfires, Hurricanes and Lancasters often flew again with swastikas painted on their tails.

With so much live weaponry in use, accidents became commonplace on both sides. Across the North Sea at the German airfield of Westerland on 16 March the bomber wing KG 30 was preparing to hit Orkney again. While the 250 kg bombs were being loaded onto the under-wing racks of the Junkers Ju-88s of No. 6 section one fell off and exploded. No less than five Junkers bombers were destroyed or badly damaged in the blast and four aircrew were killed. In the meantime, the rest of the group took off and headed north. After a long flight over the sea the bombers swooped down and, seeing Scapa Flow empty of capital ships, for the first time turned their attention to alternative targets. The raiders dropped some 117 high-explosive bombs on Orkney before running for home, losing another Junkers to anti-aircraft fire on the way. Some 31 of these bombs exploded around Bridge of Stenness. Several houses were damaged and fires started in this, the first deliberate raid on civilian targets in Britain. Two men and one woman were seriously injured and one man, twenty-seven year old James Isbister, was killed.

He was the very first civilian killed in Britain by German bombing, but unfortunately for James Isbister, this still did not qualify him for historical recognition. For some reason, the word 'mainland' began to come into play in the media as an apparently legitimate qualifying clause, and it has stayed that way ever since. Recently, a daytime television programme solemnly marked the anniversary of the 'first' British

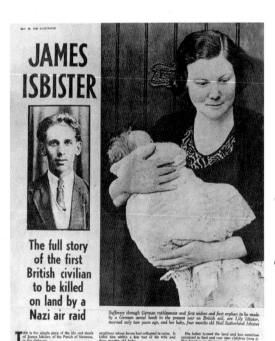

*A digitally restored cutting from the* Illustrated *magazine of 20 April 1940, which covered the story of James Isbister, the first British civilian killed by German bombing in the Second World War. Sadly, in this case, the modern British media have chosen to rewrite history in favour of events further south on the mainland.*
*(Courtesy Orkney Museum)*

civilians killed by German bombing and sent their cameras to Clacton-on-Sea in Essex, where a parachute mine had exploded on a house on 30 April 1940 (a full six weeks after the fatal Orkney raid) killing the unfortunate couple inside it. One can only wonder how the media would have dealt with the matter if the first British civilian casualty had been killed on the Isle of Wight, instead of on distant Orkney.

Shipping attacks were no longer a one-sided affair. Out in the Pentland Firth, the sailors of the Merchant Navy started hitting back. On 20 March Heinkels from 6./KG 26 got a shock when they attacked the coastal cargo ship SS *Northern Coast* south of Orkney. Hit several times by bombs, the coaster, now equipped with a couple of old Lewis guns, shot back gamely and damaged one Heinkel, which was then shot down by a Hurricane of 43 Squadron from nearby Wick. The ship's master, Captain Quirk, nursed his crippled vessel to the safety of Kirkwall Bay, where a message from RAF Wick was waiting for him: *Hearty congratulations on your courageous fight. Shout if you want us again.*

The mood would become rather more sombre two weeks later, when German bombers launched the first of several attacks around Orkney that were to grow into a series of ferocious air battles during the first half of April in support of the forthcoming German invasion of Norway. Luftwaffe aircraft roamed the northern isles attacking any ship they could find, even unarmed fishing vessels, while continuing to venture into the now very dangerous skies over Scapa Flow. The radar system and the plotting rooms were working flat-out but rose to the challenge, scrambling fighter aircraft and directing them to the right place at the right time. On 8 April three Heinkels were shot down by 43 Squadron, one even crash-landing on Wick airfield itself. Without ceremony, the two surviving crewmen were thrown into the cells at Wick police station for the night. While the imprisoned Germans pondered the start of a new life in British captivity, out on Wick airfield their crashed aircraft was stripped almost bare by eager souvenir-hunters.

When the German invasion of Norway began the following day there was an enormous amount of British naval activity around Orkney and Shetland as warships came and went to refuel, rearm and rejoin the big naval actions being fought off the Norwegian coast. Scapa Flow suddenly found itself right in the front line of the main European battlefield at that moment in history. There would be no respite for the Orkney Islands as the Luftwaffe launched one determined all-out attack after another.

But the island's defenders were ready, and at 11 a.m. that day the AA gunners at Scapa blasted a foolhardy German reconnaissance aircraft out of the sky over the Flow. After that, the waves of Luftwaffe aircraft just kept coming. Shortly after noon, a German attack was launched on a convoy in the Pentland Firth. Hurricanes from Wick were scrambled and engaged the raid in a fierce fight, losing one Hurricane in the process. Ten minutes later, another German formation attacked a battlegroup of

## PENTLAND FIRTH HURRICANE

Hawker Hurricane of No. 43 Squadron based
at Wick during the Battle of Orkney in April 1940

ships west of Orkney and was again engaged by British aircraft – on this occasion Lockheed Hudsons of Coastal Command. The same battlegroup was then attacked later in the afternoon by another German bomber force from KG 26, and once again the Hurricane pilots from Wick were scrambled to intercept and fight them off.

While this attack was taking place, nineteen more Heinkels from KG 26 set off at 1820 to attack the same fleet. Their attack caught the Wick Hurricanes in the middle of refuelling back at base, so the obsolete but still potent Gloster Gladiators from the Shetland Fighter Force were vectored south from Sumburgh by the sector radar controllers to meet this latest hostile force. The trusty old biplanes showed their worth when they successfully beat off the attack with no loss to the convoy, although one Gladiator was shot down by the bombers. Fifteen minutes after this German formation had set off, yet another large force of Heinkels took off from Westerland and headed straight for Orkney. By the time they got there it was dark. Intercepted by the exhausted British fighter pilots, two Heinkels were shot down before they reached Scapa, where a ferocious barrage of anti-aircraft explosions and searchlights lit up the sky over their target, bringing down at least one raider straight into the icy waters of the Flow. Nonetheless, the German raiders pressed home their attack with determination, hitting two cruisers and several destroyers before heading for home.

Finally, calm descended over the Orkney Islands. By the end of the day the Luftwaffe had lost almost a dozen bombers and their crews over Orkney and the Pentland Firth, with at least as many again seriously damaged and their crews wounded. These were huge air battles matching anything that would later be seen over the Channel, and they weren't over yet. Scapa Flow would see more action the following day, but by then one very major advantage had swung in the favour of the German attackers – Norway.

The distances the German aircraft would have to fly to reach their targets in Scotland had now been reduced almost by half. It made a huge difference. Stavanger-Sola was less than 300 miles from the closest landfall of Rattray Head, while most of the Shetland Islands were only a shade over 200 miles away from Bergen. The German planes could now carry more fuel or more bombs. It came as no surprise when they simply carried more of both. The north of Scotland was now about to be hit even harder.

Although another fierce day of fighting over Orkney lay ahead as dawn broke on 10 April, it was the islands themselves that opened the action, hitting back at their tormentors in dramatic style. Sixteen Fleet Air Arm Skuas from the naval air station at Hatston took off fully loaded with bombs. By the time they had returned they had sunk the German cruiser *Königsberg*, and earned the distinction of being the first aircraft in history to sink a major warship in battle.

While the Skuas landed back at Hatston, German bombers were queuing up to have a go at Orkney in formations of up to sixty aircraft at a time. Once again, the radar-directed air defences played the decisive role. Time and again the fighters at Wick and Sumburgh were scrambled and vectored to meet the incoming raids. It proved to be another hard day for both defenders and attackers, and by the end of it Orkney reeked of cordite and burning aircraft, and the inhabitants had been nearly deafened by the sound of massed anti-aircraft fire. But the system had worked. At least another ten German aircraft had been confirmed destroyed, with many more claimed as damaged and still more making crash landings back at their new Norwegian bases with dead and wounded crews aboard. Those few days in April 1940 should be named 'The Battle of Orkney'. What in effect happened was that the Luftwaffe attempted to secure air superiority over Scapa Flow, and failed. It was still officially the 'Phoney War', but these dramatic events were undoubtedly Scotland's greatest contribution to what Churchill would later call the British nation's 'finest hour'.

A few weeks after her ordeal at the hands of the German attackers, Orkney had another go at them again, sending Swordfish aircraft from Hatston to launch the first-ever torpedo attack by aircraft on a capital ship at sea. The mighty *Scharnhorst* was not sunk in the attack, but all over the world the brave effort by the Royal Navy aircrews sent a shiver up the spine of every naval officer, or at least those who had the ability to recognise the fearsome potential of this new form of attack on capital ships.

There was a pause in the action over Scotland in May and early June, as if the momentous events on the continent had caused the German forces to stop and draw breath. Dunkirk had finally been evacuated. Norway, Belgium and the Netherlands had succumbed to the invaders, while France sought an armistice, the Soviet Union helped itself to the Baltic states, and Hitler went sightseeing in newly captured Paris.

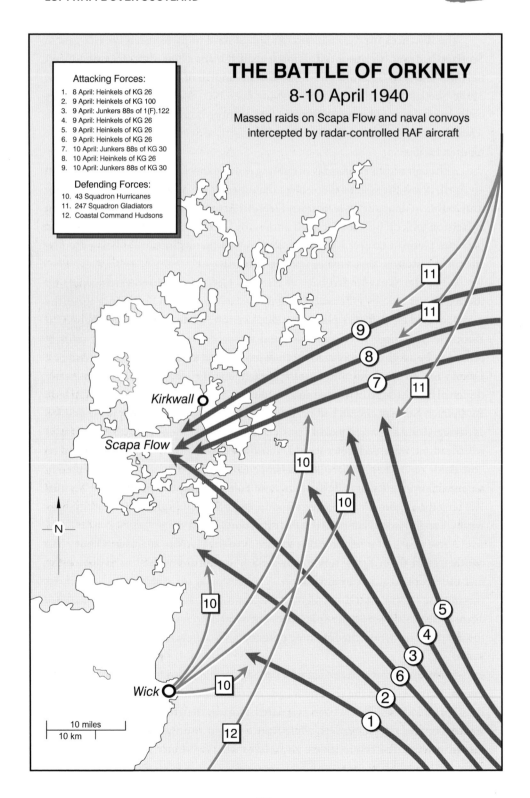

# THE BATTLE OF ORKNEY
## 8-10 April 1940

Massed raids on Scapa Flow and naval convoys
intercepted by radar-controlled RAF aircraft

**Attacking Forces:**

1. 8 April: Heinkels of KG 26
2. 9 April: Heinkels of KG 100
3. 9 April: Junkers 88s of 1(F).122
4. 9 April: Heinkels of KG 26
5. 9 April: Heinkels of KG 26
6. 9 April: Heinkels of KG 26
7. 10 April: Junkers 88s of KG 30
8. 10 April: Heinkels of KG 26
9. 10 April: Junkers 88s of KG 30

**Defending Forces:**

10. 43 Squadron Hurricanes
11. 247 Squadron Gladiators
12. Coastal Command Hudsons

Kirkwall

Scapa Flow

N

Wick

10 miles
10 km

By the time the German bombers returned to the skies of Scotland on 26 June, things had changed. Down south, the war was no longer phoney and German aircraft were now making appearances in skies that had so far never seen the Luftwaffe. The German airfleets in France and the Low Countries became the main focus of British media attention and so the new tactics of Luftflotte 5 in Norway went relatively unnoticed, except by the Scottish population, who had to endure them. These tactics became standard practice (although with some notable exceptions) for the remainder of Scotland's war. The Norway-based bombers settled into a pattern of short, fast hit-and-run attacks by either small formations of aircraft or, more usually, by single raiders. Bombers would fly in under the radar, unload a scattering of bombs on mainly coastal towns then scarper as quickly as possible before the defences could react. They were officially called 'nuisance raids' but they were in effect pure, indiscriminate terror-bombing attacks precisely in line with the Douhet theory. Sometimes the fighter defences and the anti-aircraft gunners would shoot them down; sometimes they'd never even see them.

In towns and villages all the way up the east coast of Scotland, the bombs started falling.

The first attack to have any significant effect was at Wick on 1 July. It caused a particularly dreadful tragedy for such a small town, in what has been described as the first daylight bombing raid on a British town (but only if Orkney is excluded). At 4 p.m. on a fine summer afternoon, a single Heinkel He-111 flew in under the radar and dropped its entire load on the town. At least one of its big 500 kg bombs fell among a cluster of children playing in the Bank Row area. The school holidays had been extended from 18 June to 1 October because of fears about gathering large numbers of children together, precisely to avoid what happened at Wick. But in the long summer holidays children were bound to congregate, and in Bank Row eight of them were killed while playing together. The three youngest were all aged five. Fifteen people were killed and twenty-two injured. Gas and water mains were damaged and several buildings demolished. In one family the father, son, daughter and daughter-in-law were all killed.

Despite the presence of a fighter airfield on the very edge of town and both high- and low-level radar coverage, the German aircraft was able to skim in at very low level and escape again before anyone could do anything about it. This is hardly surprising. Even today, there are few modern air defence systems that can cope with such sudden low-level air attacks. Getting in under the radar was and still is the general idea.

But even that didn't always work. In the week after the Wick attack, Scottish fighters extracted a bitter revenge on more would-be raiders by shooting down no less than seven German bombers at various locations all the way up the east coast from the Forth to Peterhead.

The pendulum of success swung the other way on 12 July, however. At 12.30 p.m., a single Heinkel He-111 of 9./KG 26 from Trondheim-Vaernes in Norway, flying in at low level to avoid the Chain Home Low radar, crossed the coast north of Aberdeen, banked to port and flew straight down the Peterhead to Aberdeen road towards the city. No siren was sounded, because radar had not detected the incoming bomber, yet somehow a scramble order was received at RAF Dyce allowing Spitfires to get airborne while the Heinkel was still approaching the city.

Two hours earlier, a separate raider had ranged across northern Aberdeenshire and for some reason selected the tiny village of Auchterless near Turriff. It dropped a single bomb on the local church manse, possibly with the intention of hitting the railway halt in the village. This would have had the Observer Corps all across Aberdeenshire watching the skies very carefully, and it is probably due to the Auchterless attack that the now-alerted Observer Corps were able to provide warning of another low-level raider in the area, this time heading straight for Aberdeen at its cruising speed of over 200 miles an hour.

The pilot, Leutnant Herbert Huck, opened up the throttles as he approached the target in order to clear the danger-zone as quickly as possible, which is evidenced by the long spread of bombs he left across the city. Hit-and-run raids were usually also hit-and-miss, but this time the bomber waited until he had Aberdeen well beneath him before releasing some twenty high-explosive bombs. It was almost inevitable that a stick of bombs landing in a fairly concentrated area of the city would find some targets, but this time almost every single bomb did exactly that. Damage was registered from King Street and Marischal Street down to the harbour area, where a bomb hit the London Boat at Waterloo Quay, and the Hall Russell & Co. shipyard was also badly hit. A group of apprentices leaving the works canteen were all killed. Four men heading for a lunchtime pint at the Neptune Bar nearby were killed in the doorway of the pub by another bomb. All across the city, blasts, shrapnel and direct hits took their toll, killing in all some thirty-four people and wounding seventy-nine others. Six houses and three factories as well as the pub were seriously damaged. Nearly a hundred other buildings suffered light damage.

The day became known as 'Black Friday' in Aberdeen, but even as the life was slipping away from those killed by the bombs, the German crew, who had caused so much death and destruction in only a matter of moments, were already facing certain death themselves. The track of the aircraft from north to south down the city along the King Street axis shows a turn to port to bring it over the shipyard and then, apparently inexplicably, a very steep turn to starboard bringing it back over the city running west along the River Dee. Inexplicably, because the first thing a hit-and-run bomber needs to do is get away again before the defences can react, and the open sea towards Norway was the other way.

The reason would have been very obvious to the bomber crew, however, when at the end of their bombing run over Footdee and the harbour they would have found themselves flying straight down the barrels of the heavy guns of the Torry Battery, which had a commanding view over the harbour. It may well be that the gunners got off a fatal shot at the bomber, but this should not denigrate the efforts of the three Spitfire pilots, who acted with incredible speed. Even as their wheels were tucking-up into their wings, the Spitfires would have been banking steeply over the city and into an attack position on the bomber.

All three Spitfires fired a long burst at the Heinkel and riddled it with De Wilde incendiary bullets from end to end. It is almost certain that somewhere over Duthie Park at 1250 hours, Leutnant Huck was dead and slumped over his controls, because the distance from the reported attacking position of the Spitfires to the crash site of the low-flying Heinkel is so short that it must have dived steeply into the ground upon being hit. The German aircraft ploughed into a new ice rink under construction in South Anderson Drive and blew up. Messrs Gilroy, Caister and Arber of 603 Squadron all took a share in the destruction of the German aircraft. The four crewmen from the bomber were buried in the old Dyce churchyard – right under the flightpath of the airfield their assassins had taken off from.

German bombers would continue to attack Scotland without let-up for the next seventeen days. One interesting raid took place at Moffat in the Borders on 20 July. This is interesting because Moffat was the birthplace of that 'greatest Englishman in history', Hugh Dowding, who was at that moment masterminding the ultimately successful air defence of Britain. Yet with this raid and so many others, the bombers were showing that there was rarely ever any co-ordinated pattern to their attacks. German raiders would rush in at low level, look for any target flashing past below them that looked big enough or important enough to bomb, let loose some or all of their load on it, then flee out to sea as fast as possible. It was a waste of effort and of lives, both in the air and on the ground, especially when the destructive power of the German raiders could so easily have been put to far better use elsewhere – on the west coast.

Without doubt, the single most tempting target in Scotland was located at Ardeer in Ayrshire. The huge ICI explosives works was a facility that the Luftwaffe knew all about, as the existence of captured German reconnaissance photographs has proved. These photographs, taken from a great height but at pin-sharp resolution, clearly show the sprawling, blast-bund protected buildings and facilities of the giant complex, which produced explosives such as RDX, Torpex and nitro-glycerine for the entire British war effort. It was the potential fireworks display to beat them all and only a few lucky bombs in the right places would have been enough to light the big blue touch paper. And yet for all the tremendous effort the Luftwaffe regularly put into pointless raids on unimportant targets, Ardeer was only attacked twice, both times in July 1940, and only as a half-hearted effort that caused no loss of production at the plant.

Hindsight is a great thing, of course, but in the same way that 'Bomber' Harris only diverted his bombers onto the key Achilles' heel target of the German petroleum industry (and then only reluctantly) when it was so late in the war as to make little difference to the outcome, one has to marvel at the incompetence of German planners in failing to launch a series of determined and devastating attacks on Ardeer. Of all the strategic targets in Scotland, this one could have been a war-winner for the Luftwaffe. Instead, the Douhet doctrine of the random killing of civilians continued to be religiously observed.

A typical example took place on 19 July, when two Dornier Do-17 aircraft attacked Glasgow at 10.13 a.m. The bombers chose an unusual approach route to their target, crossing the coast north of Aberdeen then heading south. It seemed as if the Germans were aware of an area of thin coverage provided by the CHL stations in the north-east corner. Using the Aberdeenshire gap to attack targets further south in Scotland might appear a strange ploy, but both sides knew that once the raiders

*German high-level reconnaissance photo of Scapa Flow in early 1940, prior to the Battle of Orkney. Numbers 1 to 8 indicate around a dozen Royal Navy capital ships, while 'a' shows one of the HAA batteries of this well-defended strategic naval base.*
*(Courtesy W.L.B. Stuttgart)*

*The pilot of a German Heinkel He-115 seaplane smiles confidently for the camera despite the fact that he is flying an example of the most vulnerable aircraft to appear over Scotland in wartime. This seaplane was primarily designed as a torpedo bomber, but was slow, cumbersome and therefore easily shot down. (Courtesy O.I. Vignes)*

had crossed the Scottish coast they could no longer be tracked by radar and were therefore harder to intercept.

These two raiders caused a lot of damage in the Blawarthill and Govan districts of the city, ending the lives of four people there and injuring twenty-four others. In addition, twenty-one families were rendered homeless when an entire tenement block collapsed and serious damage was done to other property. It is possible that the same two Dorniers tried the ploy again the following day, but without quite the same success, when a 603 Squadron Spitfire was scrambled early from Aberdeen to meet them out at sea. One turned back, while the other, a Dornier Do-17 P-1, flying from Stavanger-Sola was shot down off Peterhead.

Later that same day, another low-flying German raider scored an own-goal when he attacked a POW camp in the grounds of Duff House at Banff, no doubt assuming that the rows of huts he targeted were an army barracks. Six German submariners captured from the *U-27* the previous September were killed and seventeen other POWs were injured, along with two British guards. One curved wing of the historic Duff House was hit and destroyed, and so to match it the astonishing decision was taken to pull down the other wing, in an act of architectural vandalism that could not be blamed entirely on the Luftwaffe.

Meanwhile, all over eastern Scotland the hit-and-run raids continued on an almost daily basis.

By the end of July the Battle of Britain was at its height. Yet while the aircrew combatants fighting over the English Channel were being portrayed as 'knights of olde' jousting in the sky, a minor but worrying development at Peterhead on the 27th put paid to any misguided notions of chivalry that may have been lingering in

Scottish hearts. A single German bomber roared in low over the town and started blazing away at the streets below with its MG 81 machine guns, fortunately without casualties. Clearly, all pretence at decency was now gone as far as the German aircrews operating over Scotland were concerned. It was a tactic that became standard practice on all low-level German raids on Scotland and, despite post-war protestations to the contrary from German aircrews, there is such an overwhelming body of evidence from witnesses testifying to these events all over Scotland that it simply cannot be denied that indiscriminate strafing of Scottish civilians was repeatedly undertaken by the wartime Luftwaffe.

One unusual air attack on the second day of August produced an even more unusual result. A formation of Heinkel He-115 seaplanes attacked a merchant shipping convoy six miles south of Stonehaven. These twin-engine torpedo-armed aircraft were fitted with a huge pair of floats that made them slow and cumbersome. Aboard the merchant ships, the Lewis-gun-armed sailors were determined to fight back and proved as much by shooting down two of the attacking aircraft. A third Heinkel fell to a 235 Squadron Blenheim in the area, while the fourth one to be shot down could definitely be claimed by the cargo ship SS *Highlander*. Armed with a mortar-like device called a Holman projector, which used compressed air to fire a small bomb that exploded in mid-air, the sailors on *Highlander* successfully hit an attacking Heinkel, which then crashed straight onto the deck of their ship. Miraculously, neither the aircraft nor its torpedo exploded, and later that day Aberdeen was treated to the bizarre sight of a ship arriving in the harbour with a big German bomber sprawled messily all over her deck.

All through 1940 German raiders often bombed the most unlikely places in Scotland, from Tobermory on Mull to Glenkindie near Alford. One unusual target on 15 August was the big railway viaduct at Cullen, which German intelligence incorrectly identified as carrying the main Glasgow to Inverness railway line. The attacking aircraft was unusual in that it was a twin-engine Messerschmitt Bf-110 *Zerstörer* (Destroyer). It missed the target, but its presence was ironic because just up the road at Buckie, yet another Bf-110 had generated something of an enduring legend, verified by many people over the years. A Buckie fishing trawler had brought a crashed *Zerstörer* to the surface in its nets, with the remains of the dead German aircrew still aboard. This was too much for the notoriously superstitious fishermen who, refusing to sail in their by-now cursed boat ever again, pulled her up the shore and burned her.

As August gave way to September and the nights began to lengthen in Scotland, there appeared to be no let-up in the steady routine of coastal raids and offshore shipping attacks, but the first indications of a sea-change in German tactics over Scotland were about to reveal themselves. The night of 17 September saw the first of three consecutive night attacks by small raiding forces on Glasgow. Compared with the catastrophic result of raids that would be experienced along the banks of the Clyde the following year, the effects were relatively minor, although these three raids represented a significant shift of German strategy away from the half-hearted threat of invasion in the south, to the full-blooded pursuit of the Douhet theory across the entire country. If the British air force could not be defeated, perhaps her people could.

During the first raid on the 17th Glasgow was attacked four times between 1 a.m. and 4 a.m. Roads leading into Glasgow were blocked by damaged lighting cables. Tenement properties were damaged and a number of families made homeless. Of the 63 casualties inflicted, none were fatal. The second raid, on 18 September, was directly over the centre of the city and buildings were destroyed in Queen Street, John Street and North Frederick Street. The Underground at Partick was put out of action and HMS *Sussex* received a direct hit while lying at Pointhouse Quay. Although technically sunk, she was later refloated, but a total of 18 sailors aboard her were killed. The third and final night raid, as if to emphasise the sporadic nature of German bombing accuracy, recorded no material damage or casualties at all, although official concern was voiced by Glasgow City Corporation about the increasing use of parachute mines, the explosions of which, it claimed, produced an exceptionally severe blast.

For the remainder of September, the Luftwaffe contented themselves back in their usual hunting grounds on the east coast, although Oban broke the pattern by being attacked by a lone raider on the 24th of the month. One unfortunate bombing casualty at the end of September was a bonded warehouse in Dalry Road in Edinburgh, where over a million gallons of pure malt went up in flames, thanks to the Luftwaffe. Human casualties were more serious later that day in Aberdeen,

*A German parachute mine that failed to explode. This photograph shows the scale of these huge bombs. Although the hole in the side shows where the mine has been safely defused, the couple in the picture are understandably nervous about standing in their own back garden next to this monstrous device.*
*(Courtesy Liverpool Museums)*

A rare shot of one of the dreaded German parachute mines being loaded aboard a Dornier Do-217. Designed to have their descent retarded by parachute, these devices did not penetrate at high speed like a normal bomb, but instead exploded either out in the open or at a pre-set low altitude for maximum blast effect. (Courtesy Feldgrau.com)

The aftermath of a bombing raid in Peterhead on 2 October 1940. A senior police officer supervises the rescue operation to try to find survivors among the rubble, an operation that had clearly been going on for some time after the attack took place. This police officer then appears in the following photograph, which was to become one of the most famous taken in Scotland during the war. (Courtesy Aberdeen Journals Ltd)

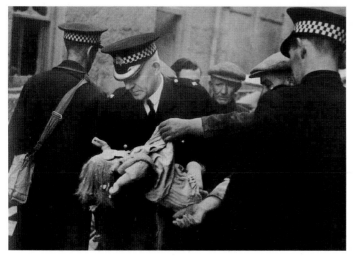

The result of the same rescue operation shown in the previous photograph. Often incorrectly stated as being taken in Clydebank, the photograph was taken in Peterhead. This type of picture would have been censored in wartime for obvious reasons. More than sixty years after it was taken, it is still a shocking image of the brutality of war and the cruelty of the Douhet theory. (Courtesy Aberdeen Journals Ltd)

when one man was killed and forty-eight others injured by a large bomb exploding in Oscar Road in the Torry area of the city. This steady pattern of random attacks resulting in civilian deaths among the citizens of east coast towns continued all through October, although it was becoming clear that night raids were also steadily increasing in intensity. As if to illustrate the growing menace of bombers operating in the darkness, it was officially noted that on the 23/24 October, practically all of Scotland was under air-raid alert.

Offshore, the stubborn Heinkel He-115 torpedo seaplanes kept on attacking convoys near Rattray Head, and kept on getting shot down for their trouble. Far more serious for the defenders, however, was a persistent increase in the number of surprise attacks on Scottish east-coast airfields. Two fighter squadrons, numbers 603 and 111, happened to be based at RAF Montrose on the day the Luftwaffe decided to try to get even with them. At 6.30 p.m. on 25 October, three German Ju-88s roared in at very low level over the airfield and scattered some twenty-four bombs, strafing heavily as they went. In the few minutes it took the raiders to clear the airfield, five RAF airmen were killed, eighteen injured and serious damage done to dozens of airfield buildings. Eight aircraft were destroyed on the ground and many more damaged. It is likely that the same three raiders were responsible for fast strafing attacks on the nearby airfields at Edzell and Arbroath, before all three escaped out to sea under cover of darkness.

This potentially serious new tactic was repeated the following day at two RAF airfields further north, and at almost exactly the same time of day, revealing a Teutonic predictability. At 1800 hours at Wick two Heinkel He-111s raced in at very low level, reportedly flashing the correct identification signals, although it is likely that this report was simply one designed to save face by the defenders. Some of the bombs dropped by the raiders overshot the airfield and exploded in a nearby council housing estate, demolishing several of them. There were fifteen civilian casualties, three of which were fatal, to add to Wick's rising wartime death toll. On the airfield, two hangars were damaged, one so severely that it remained in ruins for the rest of the war.

Half an hour later three more Heinkels arrived over the airfield at Lossiemouth. By now, however, every airfield on the east coast was on full alert for further dusk attacks, and the anti-aircraft guns were manned, loaded and ready. Two of the raiders attacked from the sea at 100 feet, while a third roared in from the west. Any attempt at careful aiming was disrupted by the barrage that came up to meet the bombers, and most bombs landed harmlessly on the edge of the airfield, although a Blenheim was hit and destroyed. Inevitably, one of the Heinkels was brought down. It crashed spectacularly right in the middle of the airfield, killing all aboard. On the ground, two RAF personnel were killed and twelve wounded. But the Luftwaffe had been rumbled with this new ploy and they knew it, never attempting the exercise again.

If anyone thought they could detect a slackening of the pace in the German attacks, they were quickly dissuaded by what was clearly a determined effort by the Luftwaffe right across Scotland in early November, with raiders attacking both the central belt and the east coasts. And yet, inevitably, the worst of the death and destruction was delivered on the north-east coast. Aberdeen repeatedly suffered casualties in random attacks, and 4 November was simply one more bad day for the city, when the crowded working-class Torry area was hit again. Three people were killed and forty-three injured in an enormous explosion on Wellington Road, which shattered nearly every window in the entire area.

The following night it was Fraserburgh that came off worst. At 7 p.m. on the 5th, a fire accidentally broke out in a large shop and spread out of control. Enemy raids had already been plotted off the coast near Edinburgh, and the light of the fire in the broch could be seen high above the Forth, drawing the German bombers northwards like moths to a flame. At 9.16 p.m., the bombs started falling across Fraserburgh town centre, with one scoring a direct hit on the crowded Commercial Bar on Kirk Brae, where a darts match was in progress. The entire building collapsed on top of the occupants. A bus to Rosehearty that was standing nearby was damaged in the blast, but still set off with a load of terrified passengers to get away from the bombing. The bus and its unfortunate passengers were caught by the blast of another very large bomb, which exploded in a field as the bus was passing Gallowhill Terrace, leaving a huge crater. More raiders appeared over Fraserburgh, yet rescue teams at the Commercial Bar kept working through the bombing and were still digging the dead out by daylight next morning.

In all, 34 people were killed and 52 others injured in Fraserburgh's worst night of the war.

The following night, a German raider headed across to the west coast and attacked Campbeltown, where children evacuated from Glasgow were being housed. In a town that could not conceive of ever being attacked there were no air-raid facilities, and there were a number of casualties when the old Royal Hotel suffered serious damage at the hands of this lone attacker. But the pace was definitely slackening.

The remaining month of the year saw only a few minor scatterings of random bombs in a number of diverse locations across Scotland, from East Linton to Fort William. Glasgow received a couple of consecutive nights of small-scale raids a few nights before Christmas, although the effects were insignificant. A few shipping attacks were also made offshore, including one at Ardmucknish Bay in Oban, where the large cargo ship SS *Breda* was sunk by a lone German raider.

It seemed as if the Luftwaffe had finally run out of steam over Scotland, and that the longest year of war her people had ever seen was finally over.

But the Luftwaffe would be back over Scotland again in the New Year, with a vengeance.

APPENDIX 1

# OTHER EVENTS:
# JANUARY TO JUNE 1940

**13 January**    Heinkel He-111 shot down by 602 Squadron Spitfire off Edinburgh.

**17 January**    Heinkel He-111 shot down by 43 Squadron Hurricane off Wick.

**19 January**    Heinkel He-111 shot down by 603 Squadron Spitfire off Aberdeen.

**22 January**    Two Heinkel He-111s attacked by 43 Squadron Hurricanes off Wick.

**9 February**    Junkers Ju-88 shot down by AA fire off north-east coast.

Shipping attacked off Peterhead by Junkers Ju-88s.

**22 February**  Heinkel He-111 shot down by 602 Squadron Spitfire near Coldingham.

**27 February**  Heinkel He-111 shot down by 609 Squadron Spitfire off Dunbar.

**7 March**     Heinkel He-111 shot down by 603 Squadron Spitfire off Aberdeen.

**8 March**     Junkers Ju-88 shot down by 111 Squadron Hurricane off Orkney.

**3 April**      Junkers Ju-88 shot down by 204 Squadron Sunderland off east coast.

Shipping attacked off Kinnaird Head by Heinkel He-111s.

**11 April**     Three Dornier Do-18s shot down by 602 Squadron Spitfires off Fraserburgh.

**25 April**     Dornier Do-18 Flying Boat shot down by 43 Squadron Hurricane off Shetland.

**4 June**      Dornier Do-18 Flying Boat shot down by 43 Squadron Hurricane off Shetland.

**26 June**     Three Heinkel He-111s shot down by 602 & 603 Squadron Spitfires off Edinburgh and Aberdeen. Raid on Tullos Farm, Nigg, Aberdeen.

**29 June**     Raid on Peterhead.

**30 June**     Raid on Aberdeen, Victoria School burned out.

APPENDIX 2

# OTHER EVENTS:
# JULY 1940

| | |
|---|---|
| 1 July | Raid on Haddington. |
| 3 July | Four Junkers Ju-88s shot down by 603 Squadron Spitfires off Aberdeenshire. |
| 4 July | Raid on Peterhead. |
| 6 July | Messerschmitt Bf-110 shot down by 603 Squadron Spitfire off Aberdeen. |
| 7 July | Junkers Ju-88 shot down by anti-aircraft fire into the Firth of Forth. |
| 8 July | Heinkel He-111 shot down by 602 Squadron Spitfire into the Firth of Forth. |
| 10 July | Raid on Tobermory, Mull. |
| 12 July | Raids on Cupar, Dunfermline and Helensburgh. |
| 13 July | Raids on Sauchie, Greenock, Gourock and Dundee. |
| 15 July | Raids on Peterhead (prison grounds), Fraserburgh, Portsoy and Banff. |
| 16 July | Heinkel He-111 shot down by 603 Squadron Spitfire off Peterhead. |
| 17 July | Raids on Auchtermuchty and Ardeer. Attack on convoy off Dundee. |
| | Heinkel He-111 shot down by 603 Squadron Spitfire off Fraserburgh. |
| 18 July | Raids on Leith docks, Burntisland, Edinburgh and RAF Montrose and on the radar station at RAF Anstruther. |
| 20 July | Raids on Ardeer, Stirling and Peterhead (Peterhead academy destroyed). |
| | Dornier Do-17 shot down by 603 Squadron Spitfire off Peterhead. |
| 22 July | Raid on Leith. |
| 23 July | Raids on Edinburgh and RAF Montrose. |

| | |
|---|---|
| **24 July** | Raid on Rolls Royce factory at Hillington. |
| | Heinkel He-111 that attacked Hillington shot down by 603 Squadron Spitfire. |
| **25 July** | Heinkel He-111 shot down by 603 Squadron Spitfire off Fraserburgh. |
| **26 July** | Raid on Kilmarnock. |
| **27 July** | Raids on Rosehearty, Fraserburgh, Elie, Kinglassie, Falkland, North Berwick and RAF Dyce. |
| **28 July** | Raids on Edinburgh, Perth and Glenkindie, Aberdeenshire. |
| **29 July** | Raids on Midlothian and Berwickshire. |
| **30 July** | Heinkel He-111 shot down by 603 Squadron Spitfire off Montrose. |

APPENDIX 3

# OTHER EVENTS:
# AUGUST 1940

**1 August**    Raids on Montrose, Dundee, Haddington, Armadale and Duns.

Junkers Ju-88 shot down by anti-aircraft fire near Edinburgh.

**4 August**    Raid on Edinburgh.

**8 August**    Raid on Gourock.

**13 August**   Raids on Aberdeen, Peterhead, Fraserburgh and St Fergus.

**14 August**   Raids on Banffshire, Kincardineshire and Montrose.

Convoy attacked off Kinnaird Head.

**15 August**   Raids on Montrose and Cullen.

Heinkel He-115 Seaplane crashed near Arbroath.

**16 August**   Raid on Montrose.

**18 August**   Raid on Montrose.

**20 August**   Raids on Edinburgh and Glasgow.

**21 August**   Raid on Hatston, Orkney.

**22 August**   Heavy offshore minelaying from Forth estuary to Kinnaird Head.

**23 August**   Raid on York Street, Peterhead.

Heinkel He-111 shot down by 232 Squadron Hurricane off Shetland.

**25 August**   Raid on Montrose.

Convoy attacked off Kinnaird Head.

Convoy attacked by U-boats off Lewis; five ships sunk.

**26 August**   Convoy attack off Rattray head; two ships sunk

**27 August**   Strafing attacks on RAF airfields at Dyce, Edzell and Montrose.

**28 August**   Raids on Fraserburgh, Peterhead, Monifieth and Aberdeen

**30 August**   Raid on Rosyth.

APPENDIX 4

# OTHER EVENTS:
# SEPTEMBER TO DECEMBER 1940

| | |
|---|---|
| 2 September | Attack on convoy off Kinnaird Head. |
| 3 September | Raids on Firth of Forth and east-coast locations. |
| 4 September | Raid on East Lothian. |
| 6 September | Raid on Kinghorn. |
| 11 September | Heinkel He-111 crashed in Moray Firth. |
| 15 September | Attack on convoy off Montrose, 2 ships sunk. |
| 16 September | Two Heinkel He-115s shot down by anti-aircraft fire off Eyemouth and Aberdour. |
| 24 September | Raids on Dundee and Oban. |
| 26 September | Convoy attacked off Firth of Forth. |
| 27 September | Convoy attacked off Montrose. |
| 28 September | Convoy attacked off Rattray Head, one ship sunk. |
| 29 September | Convoy attacked off Troup Head, two ships sunk. |
| 2 October | Raids on Glasgow, Montrose, Peterhead and Fraserburgh. |
| | Convoy attacked off Rattray Head. |
| | Heinkel He-115 shot down by 254 Squadron Blenheim over convoy. |
| 4 October | Raids on Eyemouth and Dunbar. |
| 7 October | Raids on Firth of Forth and various east-coast locations. |
| 8 October | Raid on Edinburgh. |
| | Dornier Do-17 crashed off Rattray Head after engine failure. |
| 9 October | Convoy attack off Stonehaven, one ship sunk. |
| 11 October | Junkers Ju-88 shot down by 20 OTU Wellington off Lossiemouth. |
| 14 October | Raid on Renfrew. |
| 16 October | Raids on Gourock, Arbroath and Hatston/Kirkwall. |

| | |
|---|---|
| 18 October | Raids on Crail and Null Head, Orkney. |
| 23/24 October | Raid on Gourock. |
| 25 October | Raids on Greenock, Anstruther, Kilrenny, St Andrews, Arbroath and Montrose. |
| 26 October | Raids on Ayr, Cumbernauld and Dumbarton. |
| | Heinkel He-115 seaplane shot down by 603 Squadron Spitfires off Fraserburgh. |
| 31 October | Raid on Aberdeen. |
| | Convoy attacked off Rattray Head. |
| 3 November | Raids at North Berwick, Bucksburn, Fraserburgh and Newburgh, Aberdeenshire. |
| 4 November | Raids on Aberdeen, Glasgow, Dunfermline, Edinburgh, Kelty, Dundee, Rutherglen, Coatbridge and Larbert. |
| 5 November | Raids on Dundee and Aberdeen. |
| 11 November | Convoy attacked off Aberdeen, one ship sunk. |
| 13 November | Raid on Cumbernauld. |
| | Heinkel He-115 shot down by 111 Squadron Hurricanes off Aberdeen. |
| 27 November | Raid on East Linton. |
| 29 November | Raid on Kirkconnel. |
| 26 December | Junkers Ju-88 shot down by 804 Squadron FAA Martlet over Orkney. |

# 4

## SCOTLAND'S TORMENTORS
## – THE GERMAN RAIDERS

The German Luftwaffe lost some two hundred aircraft over Scotland in the Second World War. Since the majority of these aircraft belonged to the bomber units KG 26 and KG 30, it is worth taking a look at these units in a little detail, as well as at some of the other raiders who also attacked Scotland.

The letters 'KG' stand for *Kampfgeschwader*, and although the German word *Kampf* has other meanings the translation in this case means 'Bomber', with *Geschwader* meaning 'Wing'. Unlike the Royal Air Force, which was separated into individual forces such as Bomber Command or Fighter Command, the German air force was divided into *Luftflotte* or air fleets, which were generally defined by their geographical location rather than any specific function, because the idea of an air fleet was that it was a self-contained multi-role organisation. The most significant air fleet as far as Scotland was concerned was Luftflotte 5. Created in 1940 after the German invasion of Denmark and Norway, this air fleet found itself in the ideal position to launch attacks on Scotland.

The German unit designation system within the Luftwaffe was a masterclass in mind-boggling complexity. Within each air fleet there were bomber, fighter and seaplane *Geschwadern*, among others, which also included all types of reconnaissance units. A typical *Geschwader* of bomber aircraft would be split into three and sometimes four *Gruppen* (Groups) comprising around thirty aircraft each, which were then divided into *Staffeln* (Squadrons). Each *Gruppe* was identified by a roman numeral, although the squadrons were given a standard Arabic number, and so to give an example, the second *Staffel* of the third *Gruppe* of *Kampfgeschwader 30*, for instance, would be designated '2./III/KG 30'. To further confuse the issue, each *Geschwader* would have a *Stab* (Headquarters) flight of about four aircraft, and these would be designated, for example, 'Stab/KG 30'. In addition, a unit like KG 30 would also contain an *Ergänzungs* (Replenishment) unit, providing new crews with operational 'on the job' training.

The bomber wings of KG 26 and KG 30 had both been involved in attacks on Scotland since the start of the war while operating from what (until the invasion of Norway) had been their northernmost base on German soil at Westerland on the Island of Sylt. When they moved to the airfield at Stavanger-Sola the range to Scotland was dramatically reduced, and although both units moved around Norway to airfields such as Vaernes at Trondheim, they were based for most of the war at Sola, where a large lake near the airfield also allowed the Heinkel He-115 seaplanes to operate close to this central administration facility.

*Torpedo-armed German Heinkel He-115 seaplanes like these were widely used in the anti-shipping role off the coast of Scotland and were shot down in relatively large numbers. This aircraft has had its under-surfaces crudely coated with black paint for night operations.*
*(Courtesy O.I. Vignes)*

In addition to these bomber wings, other units were regular visitors over Scotland. The *Wettererkundungsstaffeln: Wekusta*, or 'Weather Willies', as they were known in Scotland, were tasked purely with the gathering of meteorological data over enemy territory and in the main avoided getting into fights wherever possible, sacrificing bombs for fuel. Many different types of aircraft from within the German inventory were used in the *Wekustas*, which were always seen as a challenge for British pilots to shoot down, since they boldly advertised their presence in the skies over Scotland with long white contrails on clear days. Eventually, after a few Weather Willies were indeed shot down the RAF ordered them to be left alone, as the weather reports received from their intercepted radio messages proved as invaluable to the British as they did to the Germans.

Other units regularly operating over Scotland were the *Aufklärungsgruppen*, which was abbreviated to *AufklGr* in German use. These were the reconnaissance units, who usually flew their missions over enemy territory on an armed basis, and were not averse to bombing anything interesting they encountered. One of the more frequent units over Scotland was AufklGr 1(F)./106, who lost a steady stream of aircraft on a one-by-one basis, as they usually operated alone. One occasional visitor, however, was usually untouchable. These were diesel-engine Junkers Ju-86 aircraft, modified and stripped down so that they could reach a ceiling of a shade under 40,000 feet, which no standard fighter of the day could reach, although modified Spitfires could and sometimes did. Not surprisingly, the diesel aero-engines proved terribly unreliable, and the aircraft itself was unstable and hard to fly, so they were quietly dropped.

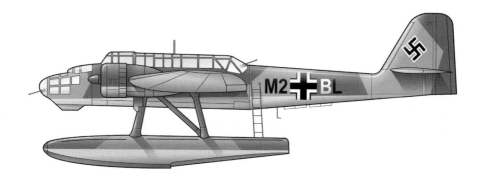

## HEINKEL HE-115 SEAPLANE

While attacking shipping off the east coast of Scotland, these slow and vulnerable aircraft were shot down regularly.

Other frequent visitors over Scotland were the Coastal Flyers, or *Kustenflieg-ergruppen*. These aircraft were nominally involved in co-operation with the German navy, but in practice tended to operate with the bomber groups of Luftflotte 5. Almost without exception, the aircraft of all these various units operating over Scotland were either Junkers Ju-88s or Heinkel He-111s. Sometimes a twin-engine Messerschmitt Bf-110 or even a single-engine Bf-109 would make the long journey over the North Sea on recce flights, but both needed to carry a lot of extra fuel in external tanks for the purpose, which made them vulnerable.

These aircraft were all designed for purely tactical short-range purposes, as was discussed in the introduction, so it was a tribute to their versatility that they could also be used in a long-range role over Scotland. The Junkers Ju-88 was the newer

Above: *Members of one very lucky Junkers Ju-88 crew from (F)./106 pose by their machine at Stavanger-Sola after returning from a reconnaissance mission over northern Scotland. In a desperate attempt to escape a pursuing RAF fighter, the pilot flew so low over the North Sea that the tips of the wooden propeller blades were sheared off. (Courtesy Olve Dybvig)*

Right: *Although Messerschmitt Bf-110 Zerstörer (Destroyers) rarely operated over Scotland, this is the type of aircraft that Deputy Führer Rudolf Hess flew to Scotland in during May 1941. (Courtesy F. Gunsche)*

of the two main types seen over Scotland. The Heinkel He-111 had seen pre-war operational use in the Spanish Civil War. This Heinkel, like many other designs from the same manufacturer, was a very graceful and sleek aircraft with a pleasing shape. It had a very distinctive all-glazed nose which, although offering the pilot outstanding visibility, gave the impression of great vulnerability too. This was illusory, however, as bullets and cannon shells could actually punch through thin aluminium aircraft skins as easily as through Plexiglas.

*This Junkers Ju-88 of KG 30, based at Stavanger, only just made it back to Norway after being damaged in one engine by anti-aircraft fire over Scotland in the winter of 1941. Frozen lakes offered a quick emergency-landing ground, and crashed German aircraft are still being recovered from Norwegian lakes to this day. (Courtesy O.I. Vignes)*

The Heinkel He-111 conformed to a standard configuration for a medium bomber, having crew access all through the fuselage and with defensive machine guns in the dorsal and ventral positions. One unique feature of the aircraft was the way the bombs were carried in the aircraft, being racked vertically with the nose at the top and the tail at the bottom. This allowed for easy in-flight arming of the nose-mounted fuses, but also meant that the bombs fell out in an ungainly way and needed quite a lot of height in order to tumble into the correct nose-down position. As we will see, the town of Fraserburgh in particular was to benefit from this on a number of occasions, with raiders releasing loads from heights of only 100 feet, which meant the bombs did not land on their noses and also did not allow windmill-type fusing devices to properly activate. Heinkels could also carry bombs externally under the wings inboard of the engines, as could their stable-mate, the Junkers Ju-88.

As we have already seen, the Ju-88 was intended as a *Schnellbomber*, but due to an unfortunate decision by Ernst Udet, was forced to be modified as a dive-bomber to the extent that this extra equipment reduced the aircraft's performance. Although the Ju-88 is nowadays lauded as one of the first true 'multi-role' aircraft (which it was)

*A German Heinkel He-111 bomber in flight. The poor defensive armament is clearly visible. The highly unpopular underbelly gun position was known as the 'coffin' by aircrews, for obvious reasons. (Author's collection)*

it is often overlooked that in its first incarnation, the A-1 version of the Ju-88 was far from a success. Chronic reliability problems with its BMW engines caused Hitler in a row with Göring in the early stages of the war to call it 'that useless Junkers eighty-eight'. But these problems were soon overcome, and the Ju-88 became a superlative and adaptable aircraft, serving as a close-support bomber on the battlefield, a fierce anti-shipping aircraft, reconnaissance aircraft, night-fighter and finally as an unmanned guided bomb in the *Mistel* configuration, which we shall meet in a later chapter.

The engineering design and manufacture of these aircraft was of a typically superior German standard, and the high build quality was always evident on closer inspection to British eyes whenever they were shot down. Part of the secret lay in good production-line manufacturing that used repeat-process jigs and tools. A good example of the importance of this is the fact that the Spitfire, often built in sections at dispersed sites, always had a 'hand-built' feel about it, with no two panel attachments ever likely to be in the same place. This exclusivity is all very well for the average luxury car connoisseur, but not so useful in combat aircraft in a wartime situation. Very rarely, for instance, would a cowling panel from one Spitfire fit another one, although they were usually always interchangeable among German aircraft types. This was important in operational use when spares or replacements had to be fitted or cannibalised from other aircraft.

*The heavy bomber that never was. The Focke-Wulf Fw-200 Condor looked the part of a heavy bomber, but because it was a converted airliner could not accommodate an internal bomb-bay and was instead relegated to long-range maritime patrol duties, where its few externally mounted bombs were used against shipping. (Courtesy Bundesarchiv Public Domain)*

Yet if they were so well made, why were German aircraft still not up to the job? As we have seen in the introduction, this was due to a disastrous pre-war decision by Albert Kesselring to cancel the German strategic bomber programme, which would have given the Luftwaffe a proper four-engine 'heavy'. The Luftwaffe, however, did in fact have a large four-engine aircraft in service from the start to the finish of the war, in the shape of the Focke-Wulf Fw-200 Condor. It certainly looked the part, so why could this particularly sleek and handsome-looking aircraft not have been used as a heavy bomber? Appearances can be deceptive, however. A heavy bomber needs one key ingredient, as any glance at British bombers like the Lancaster, Halifax and the Short Stirling will demonstrate: high-mounted wings.

British heavy bombers were all designed from the bomb-bay outwards. The first thing Roy Chadwick designed when he created the Avro Manchester/Lancaster aircraft was an immensely strong bomb-bay and wing-spar structure. Everything else was built around this, which meant that the wings had to be high-mounted on the fuselage in order to make way for the bomb bay. This is what made the Lancaster capable of carrying such enormous bomb loads for its size. With the bomb doors removed, Lancasters could carry huge outsized bombs like the 22,000 lb 'Grand Slam' earthquake bomb, or the 5 foot wide 9,250 lb 'Upkeep' bomb, more commonly known as the 'Bouncing Bomb'.

The Focke-Wulf Condor could not carry such loads because it had been designed as an airliner with a low-wing configuration, and even if a structurally strong bomb-bay could have been installed, it would not have been a big one and would not have been able to carry bombs much bigger than 500 kg. It could carry a few bombs on under-wing hardpoints to attack shipping with, but that was all. All successful heavy bombers have a high-wing configuration, although the exception would seem to be the American Boeing B-17 Flying Fortress, which also served as a heavy bomber. But once again, appearances can be deceptive.

The Fortress, for all its iconic blood-and-thunder status in American mythology, was actually rejected by the RAF as unsatisfactory for use as a bomber, which says a lot about it. Among other things, it handled very badly and was sluggish and unresponsive, and the RAF relegated the few they had to long-range coastal reconnaissance duties (which is what Germany did with the Condor). Take away the classical wartime imagery and the B-17 was essentially a low wing aircraft able to carry a relatively poor bomb-load. The most the Fortress could carry was up to three and a half tons, but this was *in total* and at the expense of fuel. In reality the B-17 could carry only a paltry two tons of bombs on operational missions. This was less than most German *tactical* bombers or aircraft like the RAF Mosquito could carry, and far less than the twin-engine German Dornier Do-217, which could carry almost four tons of bombs. The only thing the B-17 did have that the German tactical bombers did not, was height and range, And heavy defensive armament.

Although the B-17 was optimistically named the 'Flying Fortress' this most heavily self-defended of all bombers, which bristled with powerful fifty-calibre machine guns, proved decisively over Germany that bombers operating in daytime needed fighter escort and could not rely on their own defensive armament for protection from enemy fighters. German tactical bombers also carried defensive armament, but these were usually single hand-held machine guns that were often ineffective against an attacking fighter. Furthermore, German aircraft had one major weakness when it came to being attacked, whether by fighters or by anti-aircraft fire. In German bombers like the Junkers Ju-88 and most of the Dornier variants, the crew were huddled together in one central bulged area in the nose. It has long been suggested that this was in order to improve crew morale, but this seems a very curious argument.

*The most lethal German bomber was the Dornier Do-217. This aircraft was used only once against Scotland, on the last occasion when the country was bombed by the Luftwaffe during the Second World War, when a raid was mounted by KG 2 on Aberdeen and Fraserburgh in April 1943. (Author's collection)*

It is far more likely that considerations of cost, aircraft size, weight and ease of manufacture dictated this standard German layout. As we have seen, the ability to produce as many aircraft as quickly as possible was an over-riding consideration in the 1930s when the Luftwaffe was trying to build up its strength. Keeping the crew cooped-up in a relatively static set of positions in the nose area meant that the aft fuselage could be a light, narrow structure that was easier and cheaper to make than one that needed to permit crew access. This is why German aircraft have a distinctive long and thin rear fuselage, none more so than the Dornier Do-17, in which the effect is so pronounced that it was named the 'Flying Pencil'.

However, far from being good for morale, this recognisable feature of German bombers (the Heinkel He-111 was the notable exception to this layout) meant that the risk of death among the closely bunched crew when attacked was not only magnified – one burst of machine-gun fire into the cockpit could kill them all – it also meant that there was no room for the other crewmen to remove the pilot and take the controls if he was killed or wounded. Add in the fact that the hit-and-run raiders attacking the north and east coasts of Scotland flew so low that a fatal hit on the pilot was inevitably fatal to the rest of the crew, who would have neither the room inside the aircraft nor the height above the ground to do anything about it before

*A German Dornier Do-18 Flying Boat of the type used for maritime reconnaissance over Scotland. Although this aircraft wears Red Cross markings, aircraft like these were used to rescue German airmen shot down into the sea, and since rescued crews would be able to rejoin hostilities, RAF policy was always to attack these aircraft in the same way as other German aircraft, much to the fury of the Luftwaffe. (Courtesy G. Martin)*

the aircraft crashed. Some movement was possible in aircraft with an underbelly gondola, or with a forward-firing gun in the nose. These nose guns were initially standard machine guns, but were upgraded in aircraft like the Dornier Do-217 to large 20 mm cannon, and it is particularly interesting to note that these nose cannons were only capable of firing *downwards* – not upwards at attacking fighters.

Clearly, these cannons were not defensive – they were deliberately fitted for strafing.

It may seem somewhat hypocritical to condemn the fitting of these cannons in an aircraft designed to drop bombs and kill people, but the positioning of such a gun for such a purpose can only be described as barbaric. The job of the tactical bomber was to drop bombs on its target which, by definition, was usually to be found on a battlefield. But the Dornier Do-217 was designed and used *primarily* for fast and low-level bombing attacks over Britain. That being the case, the only targets that the nose-mounted cannon could possibly be used to strafe were British civilians on the streets below. There are two aspects of this policy of deliberate strafing by such large-calibre weapons that need to be considered.

The first is that the 20 mm cannon is a particularly nasty weapon, which was used to great effect in every role and theatre of the war. The high-velocity projectiles they fired were usually explosive-tipped and a hit from a single 20 mm round could blow off an aircraft's wing. When a person is hit by one they are never wounded, they are simply blown apart where they stand. In the last raid on Scotland at Aberdeen in April 1943, one of the attacking Dorniers circled the city at low level several times, deliberately strafing the streets with its 20 mm cannon, which leads to the second aspect of German strafing policy in general.

Why were the German aircrews always apparently so keen to do it?

The deliberate policy of strafing British civilians during a hit-and-run raid was one dictated by the High Command of an already murderous regime, hence the fitting of these lethal cannons solely in order to kill as many civilians as possible. But if, as we shall see in a later chapter, many German crews were often quite prepared to ditch their bombs harmlessly over open countryside in order to be able to run for home and avoid further danger, why then were so many of them equally as keen to viciously rake streets filled with innocent men, women and children with large-calibre cannon or machine-gun fire?

This seems a particularly cruel and ruthless way to fight a war against civilians. Was it perhaps seen as an extension of the Douhet theory of hitting civilian morale? One would think that, even if ordered to strafe, decent German crews would have had a sense of conscience and merely paid lip service to their orders and fired a few rounds over the heads of civilians, or even emptied their magazines out at sea in order to give the impression that they had fired them all at civilians. No one would have known. The uncomfortable truth, however, is that German aircrews strafed British streets with apparent glee – there is no other way to describe it – and any historical account of their actions must condemn them for it.

In the introduction, the desire to avoid the emotive language of wartime was expressed. Although at all times this writer has striven to describe German aircraft by every possible adjective other than the word 'Nazi', the issue of the political make-up of these German crews must at some point be addressed, if only to explain the lack of restraint when it came to strafing British civilians.

No matter how often some post-war historians may attempt to rehabilitate the Luftwaffe in terms of distancing them from Nazi atrocities, the fact remains that, with the notable exception of the SS, the air force was the most loyal among the German armed forces to the Nazi Party. The army and navy had maintained their long 'Prussian Officer' tradition of political independence, despite Hitler's rise to power.

The Luftwaffe, however, nominally headed by the figurehead of Hermann Göring, owed everything to the Nazis, who had built-up the air force in secrecy despite the restrictions of the Versailles Treaty. The Nazis filled the ranks of the air force with bright, obedient blond boys straight from the Hitler Youth, all unquestioningly indoctrinated into the party creed. These same boys went on to become the arrogant, strutting Luftwaffe officers whose attitude so enraged the British people who encountered them after they had been shot down and captured over Britain.

It should not be forgotten that every Luftwaffe aircraft carried a large swastika on its tail and, despite the efforts of some people to portray the Luftwaffe as somehow having had little to do with the Nazi political creed, the reality is that this was simply untrue – the Luftwaffe was filled with aircrews at best sympathetic towards, and at worst dedicated to, the cause that the swastika represented.

Unfortunately, nothing demonstrates this better than the hard evidence of Luftwaffe aircrews strafing innocent civilians on the streets of Scotland's towns, time and time again.

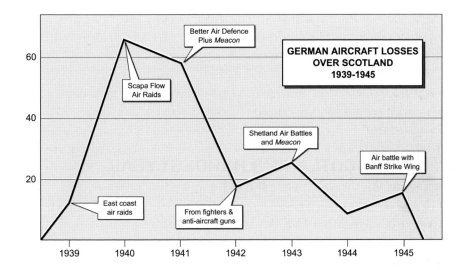

# 5

## *1941*

## SCOTLAND'S HARDEST YEAR
## PART I

In terms of civilian casualties, 1941 was by far the hardest year of war endured in Scotland.

More Scottish civilians were killed by German bombing between March and May that year than were killed during the rest of the war put together. Most of them died on the banks of the River Clyde. The pair of separate two-night raids that caused so much suffering were such calamitous events in modern Scottish history that every other wartime event in the country would seem to pale into insignificance by comparison, even though this would be an injustice to all the other casualties of German bombing in Scotland. It was a process that resumed on 7 February 1941 at Fraserburgh, where a minor miracle took place.

At noon a single Ju-88 came in fast over the town at very low level, machine-gunning everything in front of it. It dropped two large 500 kg bombs from only 100 feet. The first fell on the gasworks located at the corner of Mid Street and Finlayson Street. What happened would later become a technique known as 'skip-bombing' but it is unlikely that this is what was intended. The first bomb, maintaining the fast forward momentum of the bomber that dropped it, fell between two large gas holders, bounced up and passed clean through an upright stanchion on one of them before skipping away across a lane, through a kippering kiln and part of the works, causing a lot of damage as it went, before stopping in a corner of a yard in Albert Street without exploding. Had it done so at the point of impact, the explosion of the gasworks might have flattened half of the town. The second big bomb also failed to explode. It bounced off a road, struck a chimney at the corner of Mid Street and Charlotte Street and went through a roof, finally coming to rest in a kitchen where it injured the ankle of a Mrs Greig, who was standing at her kitchen sink.

The bomb fuses had been the standard explode-on-impact type, but because they'd been dropped from too low a height, the windmilling safety devices on the nose had not had time to prime the detonators. It seemed like an extraordinarily obvious thing for the Germans to overlook, yet precisely the same mistake was made forty years later by Argentinian Skyhawk pilots bombing Royal Navy ships at low level in the Falkland Islands. At least, it was made right up until the British media, ever impartial, reported the fact to the world and inadvertently persuaded the Argentinians to change the fuse settings on their bombs.

This failure of bombs dropped at low level to explode on impact was seen again in March just off the coast of Fraserburgh, when the Aberdeen steam trawler *St Agnes No. 1* was bombed at very low level by a German raider off Kinnaird Head. One of the bombs skipped back off the sea, went straight through the wheelhouse, where it killed two crewmen, then passed out the other side into the sea without exploding. It was obvious to the German crews that the fuse settings on their bombs had to be changed, but in so doing the bomber crews who undertook low-level attacks were placing themselves in real danger from their own bombs. The aforementioned safety devices were precisely that, designed to ensure a bomb did not explode near the aircraft delivering it. Removing them meant that raiders dropping fully primed bombs at very low altitudes would be in danger of being blown to pieces by the explosions of their own bombs.

Meantime, enemy bombers continued to prowl around their usual haunts off the Scottish east coast, bombing and strafing whatever they could find. But this practice was about to change.

On the night of 13/14 March, the Luftwaffe launched their first attack on a target they had given the codename 'Gregor': a target that was otherwise known as Clydebank.

British cities were by then being pounded nightly by massed German bomber formations in a sustained attack now collectively known as the Blitz. This was the Douhet theory being tested for all it was worth by the Luftwaffe, and it was still unclear if the British civilian population would be able to take it. Mercifully, Scotland had not been hit so far by a raid of this magnitude, but few were in any doubt that it was coming. Most people expected the blow to fall on the bigger population centres of either Glasgow or Edinburgh. Clydebank seemed an unlikely candidate for the honour. In 1941, the town had yet to merge into the modern conurbation that is greater Glasgow and like so many other industrial towns around Clydeside, still stood physically apart from its neighbours. Dominated by shipbuilding yards and

A superb shot of a Lockheed Hudson of 220 Squadron based at RAF Wick taken on 27 August 1941. These widely used Coastal Command aircraft remain relatively unsung, although while operating from airfields in the north and east of Scotland they often performed in the role of fighters instead of maritime patrol aircraft, shooting down many German aircraft during the course of the war. (Courtesy F.E. Clarke Collection)

Unlike the German medium bombers that attacked Clydebank, British heavy bombers like the Avro Lancaster could deliver a massive bomb-load such as the fourteen 1,000 lb bombs shown here and more. Had German aircraft been able to carry this type of enormous bomb-load, the casualty figures inflicted in the Clydeside and Glasgow areas during 1941 would have been far higher than they actually were. (Courtesy Life/US National Archives)

the huge Singer sewing machine factory, Clydebank boasted a pre-war population of some 50,000 people, which had been swollen to around 60,000 by the demands of war production in the bustling industries of the town.

*By contrast with the British Lancaster, the bomb bay of Germany's best load-carrying bomber for most of the war, the Dornier Do-217, seems tiny by comparison. This difference in bomb-delivery capability was a major factor in the comparable effects of the bombing campaigns mounted by the Germans and the Allies. (Courtesy O.I. Vignes)*

Yet here is the evidence that German planners had chosen this industrial target for its strategic importance alone. Target photographs found after the war clearly show that the Germans identified the many facilities at Clydebank and intended *primarily* to attack these, rather than just the civilian population. The huge admiralty oil tank farm at Dalnottar was specifically marked for German navigators to attack, as was the vast Singer factory, which was by that time manufacturing war materials and components. And of course, so too was one of the most famous shipyards in the world – John Brown & Company. The unfortunate fact that in Clydebank these important national facilities sat cheek-by-jowl with densely packed workers' tenement housing was (for the Germans) incidental to the main purpose of their mission, which was to attack strategic armaments and shipbuilding facilities. What happened at Clydebank still sends a shiver up the collective Scottish spine, but it

*The crew of a KG 26 Heinkel He-111 pose with their mascot, a lion cub. The wing was named the 'Lion'*
*Geschwader, and although the wing normally attacked Scotland from their bases in Norway, elements of KG*
*26 relocated to northern France to take part in the Clydebank raid of March 1941.*
*(Courtesy Feldgrau.com)*

cannot be denied that, unlike raids such as the Allied attack on Dresden, the first
night of the Clydebank attack was intended as a strategic attack on key industrial
facilities and not undertaken purely as a terror raid on civilians alone, regardless of
having achieved this very effect.

It has often been suggested that the raid on Clydebank was a secondary option
available to the German crews tasked with bombing Liverpool, which had been
bombed the night before, but this was definitely not the case. On the night of 13/14
March, Clydebank was the primary target of the bombers, who used an approach
to Liverpool to disguise their planned objective, as we'll see. The German bombers
were, for the moment, the masters of night-time attacks and always set out with clear
target objectives. The main attacking force was Luftflotte 3, based in France, although
bomber groups such as Scotland's old foes in the shape of KG 26 also participated.

Their tactics were by now tried and tested. Instead of the bomber 'stream'
favoured later by the RAF, German bomber formations employed a multi-directional
approach to their targets in order to confuse the defences, calling it the 'all points of
the compass' approach. This technique required the attacking force to be divided into
three or four waves, each timed to arrive over the target from different directions and
at different times in order to avoid collisions. Consequently, the first Clydebank raid
was divided into three waves, each over an hour apart, which tormented survivors
on the ground who assumed that the break between each one meant that the raid

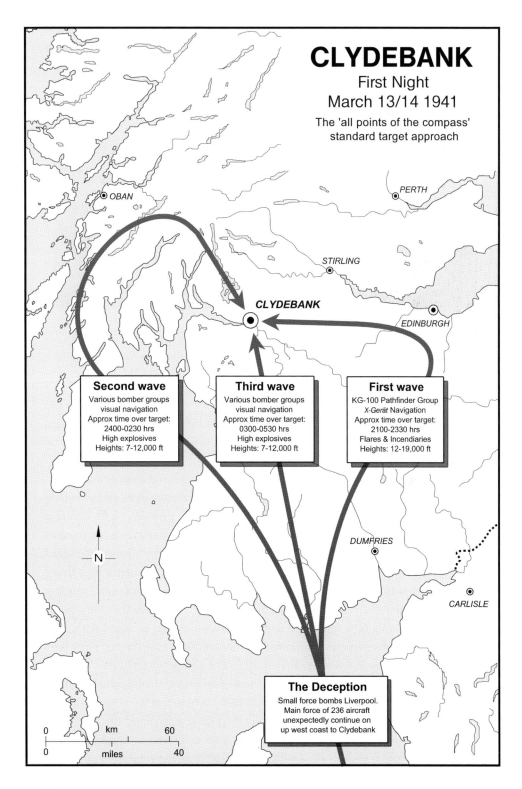

# CLYDEBANK
## First Night
## March 13/14 1941

The 'all points of the compass'
standard target approach

PERTH

OBAN

STIRLING

CLYDEBANK

EDINBURGH

**Second wave**
Various bomber groups
visual navigation
Approx time over target:
2400-0230 hrs
High explosives
Heights: 7-12,000 ft

**Third wave**
Various bomber groups
visual navigation
Approx time over target:
0300-0530 hrs
High explosives
Heights: 7-12,000 ft

**First wave**
KG-100 Pathfinder Group
*X-Gerät* Navigation
Approx time over target:
2100-2330 hrs
Flares & Incendiaries
Heights: 12-19,000 ft

DUMFRIES

N

CARLISLE

**The Deception**
Small force bombs Liverpool.
Main force of 236 aircraft
unexpectedly continue on
up west coast to Clydebank

| 0 | km | 60 |

| 0 | miles | 40 |

*Visibility from the glazed nose of a Heinkel He-111 bomber was excellent, and together with the bright moonlit conditions over Scotland on the night of the first Clydebank raid, navigators of the He-111-equipped special pathfinder wing KG 100 had little difficulty in locating the target on the distinctive River Clyde. (Author's collection)*

was over when it was not. The force that set out on the first night was estimated to comprise some 236 aircraft drawn from a wide variety of bomber groups, but headed by one in particular, Kampfgeschwader 100, the Luftwaffe's elite pathfinder force, who would lead the attack.

Deception in any bombing attack was vital in order to avoid alerting defences at the actual target, or even to have them stand down if a raid appeared to be heading elsewhere. Because Liverpool had been heavily raided the previous night, the large force that flew up the west coast of Britain that night was assumed to be returning to the same city. Defences were alerted accordingly. But while some aircraft did indeed bomb Liverpool, the main first-wave force of around eighty bombers kept flying north. Somewhere over the Borders, the formation steered north-east, heading straight for Edinburgh, where the alarms began to wail. Once again the ruse worked and the bombers, by now filling the night sky over southern Scotland with their deafening massed drone, flew close enough to the capital to cause the outer defences to open up on the raiders overhead. Then the force abruptly turned due west and headed for the Glasgow area. The bombers would now be over the surprised defences of their primary target in less than fifteen minutes.

Another important factor that confirms the primary nature of the target that night was the need for the German navigational system to have been set up well in advance. The *X-Gerät* system was a network of directional radio beams transmitted over Britain from stations on the continent. At various points these beams overlapped, and the signal the German navigators heard when this happened told them where they were, or when to open their bomb doors, or when to release their bombs. It was a crude system that would eventually be jammed and sometimes even deliberately bent by British countermeasures like *Meacon*, but for now, it worked, and would allow bombers to get close enough to their targets to allow visual confirmation if required and if indeed possible. On this particular night, visual confirmation was not merely possible, it was excellent. Scotland bathed beneath clear skies and a dazzling silver moon. Blackout or not, the landscape below would have appeared as clear as day to the German crews, with the distinctive curves and twists of the River Clyde standing out like a shining silver ribbon in the moonlight. It looked like the bombers couldn't miss, but a surprising number of them did.

The phenomenon the German bomb-aimers succumbed to was one later named 'creep-back'. This was a simple animal instinct known as fear, and came about when the terrified crew of a bomber, high over enemy territory and being shot at and sur-rounded by exploding anti-aircraft shells, felt the need to drop their bomb-loads as soon as humanly possible and get away from the danger. More often than not, most bomb-aimers would drop their loads far too early, and the damage caused below would creep back from the target in the direction of the approaching bombers. The prob-lem became so bad in the RAF that bomber crews were forced to bring back a photo to prove they had dropped their bombs on target, otherwise they were punished by having the operation removed from the tally of 30 combat missions they were obliged to fly. German bomber crews never had such penalties to worry about and the gen-eral attitude about dropping their bombs early was one of 'Who will know anyway?' Nonetheless, many German crews were more conscientious and determined about the job they had volunteered to do. When the guns opened up around Glasgow, the men were quickly separated from the boys among the bomber crews.

A measure of the level of barrage that a city's defences have put up can be determined by the amount of creep-back each raid produces. When one considers that the anti-aircraft batteries around Glasgow received less than fifteen minutes' warning of the approaching attack (on the eastern outskirts it was nearer five minutes), the effectiveness of their response has to be admired. At around 9 p.m. German crews began releasing their bomb-loads as far away as Cumbernauld. All across Glasgow, early releases fell in districts of the city well away from the main aiming point at Clydebank. This was why the elite pathfinder bombers of KG 100 were so important that night over Clydebank, where their job was to find the target with their *X-Gerät* equipment, then set it alight with flares and incendiary bombs for the following waves who were to bomb it by visual means alone. The incendiary bombs that KG 100 carried burned at over 5,000 degrees and were very good at what they were designed for – setting fire to buildings. Within that crucial first half-hour

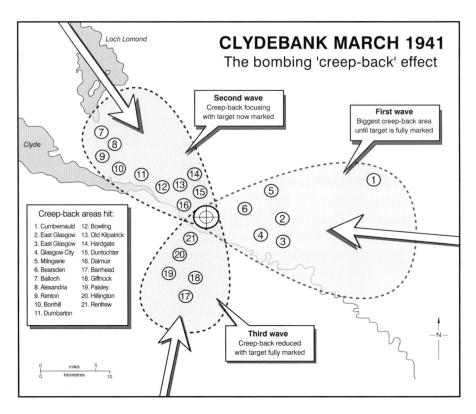

of the raid, two distilleries had been set ablaze, their whisky burning furiously. The timber yard at Singer was also well alight, as was the biggest prize of them all, the big oil storage tanks at Dalnottar, which were to burn out of control for days. The target was now marked precisely for every other bomber to see. Clydebank had become a glowing beacon of flame in the vast night sky and the fate of the town and its people were sealed. A rain of high-explosives now fell from the sky onto Clydebank.

Heavily laden bombers leapt upwards in the air as their 2 tonne cargoes fell out. High above the crowded rows of working-class tenements, scores of similar bomb-loads tumbled out, primed themselves to explode, then screamed down to detonate among houses, streets, factories, cinemas and hundreds upon hundreds of people below. Whole streets blew up. Debris lanced out in every direction, scything down anything in its path. Flame and smoke leapt out of the landscape like a scene from Hell itself.

By the time the first wave droned off, hundreds of people were already dead and the emergency services were quickly overwhelmed. A major emergency control room was destroyed. Communications were broken. Fire stations and their pumps were hit, their crews killed. Streets were blocked by fallen buildings, water mains were broken, fire hoses dribbled dry, gas mains fractured and burned, power was cut off, casualties mounted and the dead piled up.

Meanwhile, away to the north-west near Oban, the bombers of the second wave were already banking to starboard in their final waypoint turn to target.

This large formation made its approach to Clydebank by flying right down Loch Lomond and arrived over the target at around midnight. This time the aircraft were bombing visually under excellent conditions, with a brightly burning landmark to aim for. But still a great many bombers released their loads early. These bomb-loads were now exclusively high-explosives, and were dropped as far away as Balloch on the shores of Loch Lomond and on a long carpet of locations pointing like an arrow towards Clydebank. Clearly, the German bomber crews were having a hard time of it over the west of Scotland.

In Glasgow the creep-back had started numerous separate fires, which were occupying most of the city's fire-fighting resources, meaning little help could be spared for Clydebank. At around 3 a.m. the third and final wave of German bombers swept in over the target from almost due south, once more releasing a stream of early bomb-loads that marked the line of approach from Barrhead up to Renfrew.

At around 5.30 a.m. on the 14th the last bomber cleared the skies over Clydebank. An hour later, the all-clear sounded. When daybreak came, it revealed an apocalyptic scene along the banks of the River Clyde.

By early morning, news had spread of a calamity at Clydebank on a scale not yet seen in Scotland. Because the fires in the greater Glasgow area were widespread and scattered, they were brought under control more quickly and emergency teams could be sent off to Clydebank, where an almost lunar landscape of devastation awaited their eyes. Buildings everywhere lay crumpled, blackened and burning. Tramcars and buses stood gutted and twisted on the deeply cratered streets. Power lines lay down everywhere, and all around stumbled the blackened, choking, bleeding and dazed survivors. Determined rescue teams tore at the hot rubble with their bare hands when all else failed. Photographers captured scenes that even today have the power to shock. For a generation of Scots who lived through it, the images are seared into their very consciousness: the smouldering rubble field around Radnor Park; the white La Scala cinema undamaged among the smoke and the ruins; a tough, stony-faced fireman cradling a dazed young child in his arms; a thousand untold stories of suffering. Shock and loss hung like a long, silent wail of grief in the smoke-filled air. All around lay the charred evidence of human civilisation at its worst. Amid the carnage, civilisation at its best did everything it possibly could to help. They would not stop until the job was done, even when the bombers came back.

One of the great cruelties perpetrated by military leaders in the Second World War was their willingness to deliberately hit civilians when they were at their most vulnerable. Bombing a shattered, broken town while its people were still trying to recover from the first blow was one such cruelty. Each side did the same, because the

*Part of the giant Singer factory complex at Clydebank as it looked some time after the raids of March 1941. In the middle foreground, two YMCA canteen vans serve food. Beyond stand rows of what appear to be brand-new air raid shelters. Just visible at the top left is the white La Scala cinema, undamaged in the raids. (Glasgow City Archives)*

Douhet theory demanded that it be done – civilians had to be hit hard for the theory to have any chance of working.

Any possible benefit-of-the-doubt that the Luftwaffe might have been allowed for the strategic purpose of the first night's raid on Clydebank was negated by the cruel and needless raid on the second night. Fortunately, this follow-up raid was what the authorities had been expecting and many more casualties were avoided when almost all the remaining population were evacuated by 6 p.m. The only sort of people that were now likely to be killed were the ones that the Douhet devotees were most keen to see killed anyway – the skilled emergency workers, who were impossible to replace. Once more Clydebank endured the rain of high-explosive bombs, although on a slightly lesser scale on this second night, since KG 100 were not needed to mark the funeral pyre this time.

By the morning of the 15th Clydebank's agony was over, although in much the same way as the agony of a soldier can be said to be over after the shell or the sword has maimed him but spared him. Finally, the dead could be recovered and given a proper burial, or at least, those who could be found.

At first the authorities were anxious to play down the casualty figures, because as Douhet had specified, morale was the key factor in all of this. But the evidence was plain to see that a great number of people must have died. The sheer number of stunned evacuees pouring out of Clydebank spoke more eloquently than words needed to. Although 15,000 people were evacuated by the authorities after the first night attack, some 25,000 other people had evacuated themselves by the evening of Saturday, 15 March. This represented around four-fifths of the pre-war population of Clydebank. All told, some 55,000 people were made homeless in the combined Clydebank and greater Glasgow areas. The list of homes, factories and other buildings destroyed or partially ruined was enormous. All told, some 4,300 houses were demolished, either by bombs or pulled down because they were so badly ruined. In Clydebank, the official report states that only 12 houses remained undamaged in the town. It took decades to rebuild Clydebank; to fill in the gaps in the streets where once had stood a house, or an entire street of houses, or where once a family, or even an entire street of families, had been wiped from the face of the earth.

At a stroke, Scotland's civilian casualty figures rocketed. As stated previously, although the bulk of the material damage was concentrated on Clydebank, the number of deaths and injuries in the greater Glasgow area was almost twice that suffered in the town that had been the focus of the attack. Increasingly, the figure of *at least* 1,300 dead for the two-night raid has to be considered a realistic one. In truth, we'll never really know. It was wartime, and missing people were often never accounted for or never seen again. The only possible reaction to it all was shock, followed by anger.

Scotsmen fighting in every corner of the globe now had a distinct, identifiably Scottish cause to fight for. The name of Clydebank now stood alongside Coventry, Birmingham and London – names that had became synonymous with German barbarity over Britain. Scots men and women chalked the name of Clydebank onto bombs destined for German cities, or shells ready to be fired at German ships at sea.

Revenge was what people spoke about. They would not forget Clydebank, nor could they be expected to. We generations born long after these events should not condemn them for it. But if any proof were needed that Douhet's theory could induce precisely the opposite effect on a population than that intended, there was no better example than the anger that welled-up in Scots' hearts after Clydebank.

Nor should we condemn the RAF bomber crews who fully extracted that revenge from German cities to an increasingly awesome degree as the war progressed. Like

## CLYDEBANK PATHFINDER

Heinkel He-111 of Kampfgeschwader 100
One of the *X-Gerät* equipped target-finder aircraft
which led the attack on Clydebank on 13–15 March 1941

the German bomber crews, they bombed where they were told, although many RAF men began to have deep misgivings about it all.

Similarly it does not necessarily follow that because of Clydebank, people in Scotland continued to support the Allied bombing campaign over Germany, particularly after it became clear that it was getting completely out of hand. The catastrophe at Hamburg was hardly met with wild cheering in the streets of Scotland; quite the reverse. Perhaps understandably, those who had directly experienced a bombing attack like Clydebank were among those with the greatest concerns about what was happening to German cities, whether these were enemy cities or not.

This was the fundamental human difference between those who ordered the bombing raids and those who suffered underneath them. People in Clydebank who had been bombed wanted revenge in the form of winning the war, but they did not necessarily want more misery from the air inflicted upon anyone else. It was a difference in attitude that military leaders like Harris simply could not see.

Douhet, however, was by now becoming rapidly discredited, in theory, if not in practice.

*A typical scene on the streets of Clydebank following the two-night raid in March 1941. The rubble-filled streets hampered rescue efforts after the fires had been put out. In the background the fires continuing to burn at the oil storage tank farm at Dalnottar can be clearly seen.*
*(Courtesy West Dunbartonshire Council)*

In the cold language of the analysts of death and destruction, the figures were not stacking-up as hoped for. Before the war, bombing devotees had predicted a kill-ratio of fifty casualties per ton of bombs dropped. So far, the ratio was only five deaths per ton of bombs, and the people were clearly not losing their morale, they were simply getting toughened to it and motivated to fight on even harder because of it.

But it was still only March, and the agony of 1941 was a long way from being over.

APPENDIX 1

# OTHER EVENTS:
# JANUARY TO MARCH 1941

| | |
|---|---|
| **17 January** | Heinkel He-111 shot down by 3 Squadron Hurricane off Shetland. |
| **20 January** | Heinkel He-111 shot down by 43 Squadron Hurricane in North Sea. |
| **9 February** | Raid on Campbeltown. |
| **12 February** | Junkers Ju-88 shot down by anti-aircraft fire off east coast. |
| **13 February** | Raids on Aberdeen and power station at Foyers, Inverness-shire. |
| | Junkers Ju-88 crashed near Monifieth, Dundee. |
| **14 February** | Raid on Rosehearty |
| **15 February** | Raid on Invergordon naval base. |
| **17 February** | Raid on Lerwick, Shetland. |
| **19 February** | Raids on Portknockie, Fraserburgh and RAF Montrose. |
| **20 February** | Heinkel He-111 shot down by anti-aircraft fire from SS *Stella Rigler* in North Sea. |
| **22 February** | Raid on Portsoy. |
| **23 February** | Heinkel He-115 shot down by anti-aircraft fire off east coast. |
| **1 March** | Raid on Banff. |
| | Heinkel He-115 shot down by anti-aircraft fire at Whitehills, Banffshire. |
| **2 March** | Raid on Lerwick. |
| **3 March** | Raid on Haddington. |
| **4 March** | Junkers Ju-88 shot down by 253 Squadron Hurricanes at Scapa Flow. |
| **7 March** | Raid on Peterhead. |
| | Heinkel He-111 crashed during convoy attack at near Buddon, Tay Estuary |
| **8 March** | Raid on Crail, Fife. |
| **11 March** | Heinkel He-111 shot down by anti-aircraft fire off west coast near Oban. |

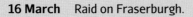

| | |
|---|---|
| **16 March** | Raid on Fraserburgh. |
| **17 March** | Raid on Wick. |
| **19 March** | Raid on Rosehearty. |
| **23 March** | Messerschmitt Bf-110 shot down by anti-aircraft fire over Sullom Voe. |
| **31 March** | Junkers Ju-88 shot down by British fighter off Peterhead. |

# 6

## *1941*

## SCOTLAND'S HARDEST YEAR
## PART II

If Clydebank could be said to have suffered a massive hammer blow, then by contrast the smaller east-coast towns continued to endure an endless succession of short, sharp stab wounds.

There seemed to be no end to the lone raiders racing in at low level, scattering their bombs on people who barely had time to look up at the sound of a fast-approaching aircraft before being knocked off their feet or killed by blast and flying shrapnel. In addition, there was the vicious machine-gun strafing from the raiders to contend with. For the population of eastern Scotland, it seemed as if hardly a single day went by without an air raid, a shipping strike or an air battle, especially around Hellfire Corner.

The day after the last Clydebank raid, Fraserburgh was attacked; then Wick; then Rosehearty; then Cruden Bay. Towns and villages with almost no relevance to the war continued to suffer fleeting attacks day after day. Most of the time damage was minimal and the casualties light. Between the raids RAF fighters and anti-aircraft artillery continued to bring down a steady toll of raiders off the coasts.

If any of this death and destruction was having any influence on the war, it was hard to see how.

Fraserburgh was attacked again on 4 and 5 April, benefiting on the second day from some good fortune – and the continuing failure of German bombs to fuse themselves. That day a single Heinkel He-111 made an attack on the Maconochie

Brothers' food factory, where the famous Pan Yan pickle was made. One 500 kg bomb exploded at the main gate. The second slammed through the stores building then skidded along for 70 yards inside it, before coming to a halt without exploding in a large kitchen area where over 100 women were working. Understandably, they panicked. The first bomb had blown in all the windows, damaged around 80 other properties in the town and put the fear of death into these women, who injured and lacerated themselves in a mass stampede through the shattered windows. In all, 6 people died and 126 others were injured. But for a badly fused bomb, it could have been an awful lot worse.

A couple of days later the sirens wailed again over the River Clyde, where numerous locations received randomly dropped bombs, including Clydebank. April, however, saw an apparently determined effort by the Luftwaffe to terrorise the people of Fraserburgh. Twice more before the month was out raiders launched a fast, brutal attack on the town. On the 17th Fraserburgh suffered the only daylight attack in Britain that day. At 3.22 p.m. a single raider skimmed in at low level without warning and dropped two 500 kg bombs in Castle Street. This time the bombs detonated, demolishing two houses and trapping the occupants inside them for several hours. Eight people were killed, including five-year-old Millicent Dunbar, who died from her injuries in Aberdeen's children's hospital the following day. Whether she understood why these terrible things were happening will never be known, nor whether the German crew had any inkling that the only thing their long flight across the North Sea had achieved was the needless deaths and suffering of innocent women and children. Twenty-nine other people were injured and ninety houses damaged in the blasts of these big bombs, which were possibly intended for the Maconochie's factory once again.

The bombers came back on the 20th, dropping a stick of nine bombs that started at the gut factory on the edge of town and formed a path of destruction along the Marconi Road area. Although the air raid sirens in Fraserburgh now traditionally sounded as the bombers were heading away, the ground defences opened up and gave the raider a hard time over the town. Ten people were injured and forty-five properties were damaged.

On the same day, another bomber headed down the coast to Aberdeen, where yet another child, three-year-old Alistair Watson, became another death statistic along with two of his relatives when bombs fell across Gallowhill, Park Road and Urquhart Road in the city.

These raiders were all operating alone, with no co-ordinated purpose to their attacks. The greatest success the Luftwaffe had achieved over Scotland so far had been when they gathered almost three hundred bombers together, divided them into three waves, then launched a concentrated two-night attack on a target that could be easily identified at night, thanks to the distinctive contours of the River Clyde.

It seemed inevitable that they would try the same thing all over again.

In early May another target on the Clyde was selected for a massed night attack – Greenock.

The entire pattern of attack, the routes and approaches of the three separate waves, as well as the target marking, was nearly identical to that executed over Clydebank. Due to Greenock's location further away from Glasgow, however, the creep-back effect would not endanger the city as much as the Clydebank attack had done. Like Clydebank, Greenock was an important maritime and military facility, with a big naval seaplane base there as well as its shipyard facilities and a torpedo factory. It was a legitimate strategic target, although once again this target was surrounded by workers' houses – workers and their families who would suffer most as a direct result of it. The attack was once again carried out by the aircraft of Luftflotte 3, based in northern France, who sent off over 250 bombers on the nights of 5/6 May and 6/7 May.

This time, however, things would work out rather differently.

First of all, the Clydebank raid was still only some six weeks in the past. The memories were not just raw; they were still hot to the touch. Improvements had been made, in attitudes as well as in defences. People were more prepared to listen and do what they were told at the first hint of an attack. Much more importantly, during the Greenock raids there were three vital factors that helped save the population from the same level of death and destruction seen up the river at Clydebank.

The first was a large decoy site built by the Air Ministry on open moorland behind Loch Thom, which was stacked high with combustible materials of every type. It was lit as the raid began and it worked. Scores of bombers were happy to deposit their bombs harmlessly onto this decoy and escape the ferocious anti-aircraft fire that was lighting up the sky over Greenock. The second big lifesaver was a network of tunnels at the east end of town where the population took shelter from the bombs. Those bombs still managed to inflict steep casualties over the course of the two nights, with the second night being the worst of the two. Bombs fell all over the town and surrounding area, with serious damage being inflicted on East Crawford Street and Belville Street. In Ingleston Street a distillery had been set alight, providing a huge fire that acted as a rival beacon to the decoy site for the rest of the bomber force.

Over the two nights 280 people were killed and over 1,200 injured. From a total of 18,000 homes, nearly 10,000 suffered damage and 1,000 were destroyed. In Paisley, a direct hit on First Aid Post No. 5 (West), by what is believed to have been a parachute mine, killed some 92 people in an instant.

Despite all this the attack on Greenock had to be considered a failure for the Luftwaffe.

The total number of civilian deaths on the ground was almost half the number of aircraft that took part over the two-night period of the raid, which roughly equates to

*Bomb damage in Belville Street in Greenock following the two night raid in May 1941. Quite often, such damage caused structural failure in the otherwise untouched neighbouring properties, which had to be pulled down. The subsequent gaps in rows of buildings often lay empty for many years afterwards.*
*(Courtesy Speirs family archive)*

a kill-ratio of one person killed for every *four* tons of bombs dropped. The advocates of air bombing were being ridiculed by such statistics.

So why did it all go so wrong for the Luftwaffe this time?

The reason was the third factor that saved Greenock that night, and it is one that has never been properly recognised. The evidence of its effect can be found in one aspect of the raid that is very clear – bomb-loads were dropped on a huge geographical area, stretching from Kilmarnock up to Dunoon and as far east as Edinburgh. It led the authorities to conclude that these were all separate raids. They were not. Greenock was the sole target, nowhere else. But although we have already seen how German bomber crews were quite happy to jettison their bombs early in order to get out of trouble quickly, this still does not explain the huge geographical scattering of aircraft and their bomb-loads during this raid.

The answer lies in the great unsung hero of the Greenock Blitz – a unique single-engine fighter named the Boulton Paul Defiant, and an aircraft that has been unjustly consigned to history as a dud.

*Intense activity in Cathcart Street, Greenock as fire and rescue crews clear rubble and search for survivors where two properties have burnedout and collapsed following the first night raid in May 1941. (Courtesy Speirs family archive)*

*A Boulton Paul Defiant night-fighter of 410 Squadron seen at Drem in September 1940. After being transferred to the night-fighter role, these aircraft were painted all over black and had their roundels painted out as well. Similar Defiants from 141 Squadron played the decisive role over Greenock in May 1941. (Courtesy 410 Squadron Association)*

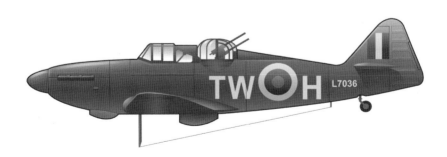

## THE NIGHT GUARDIANS OF GREENOCK

Boulton Paul Defiant night-fighter
141 Squadron based at RAF Ayr in May 1941

This fighter had proved such a woeful failure in the Battle of Britain during daytime operations that it had to be withdrawn from front-line service. Unlike conventional fighters, the Defiant had no forward-firing guns, but was instead equipped with a four-gun rotating turret like that found on bombers. As soon as German fighter pilots over the Channel understood this, the Defiants were mauled by the Luftwaffe Messerschmitts and quickly pulled out of the order of battle in southern England.

A Squadron of Defiants had been moved north to the airfield at Ayr to convert into the night-fighter role (which the Defiant was much better suited to) and were therefore in a perfect position to disrupt the Greenock raid with their now black-painted aircraft. The Clydebank raid, by contrast, had faced no such night-fighter opposition. Over the course of the two-night Greenock raid, number 141 Squadron at Ayr claimed two Junkers Ju-88s and a Heinkel He-111 as destroyed. But this modest kill rate hides the greatest success that the Defiants achieved against the Greenock raiders.

They transformed the entire situation. Mingling among the bombers, they harassed them with their very presence, forcing them to scatter all over southern Scotland, abandon their bomb-loads and race for home. The Defiants from Ayr may not have brought down many bombers, but they had fully redeemed themselves in combat. They should build a statue of a Defiant in Greenock. They were the vital factor in sparing Greenock and its population from the worst that the Luftwaffe were capable of doing to it, by breaking up the raid before it could reach its target and concentrate its bombing pattern on the town.

And thanks to the Defiant, never again would German bombers feel safe over Scotland at night.

Three nights after the last bomber departed the skies over Greenock a twin-engine German aircraft flew in over southern Scotland on the night of 10/11 May looking for a specific location, but failed to find it. Inside the Messerschmitt Bf-110 the pilot tried in vain to find where he was but, knowing he was running out of fuel, decided to bail out. His name was Rudolf Hess, and much has since been written about that famous lone flight to Scotland – some of it intriguing, some of it pure fantasy. One of the best 'incidental' stories that does the rounds in aviation circles is the RAF Acklington one. At this airfield in Northumberland, it has been claimed that one night soon after Hess arrived in Scotland, a German Ju-88 was seen to land and taxi to a far corner of the airfield. Here it was met by some waiting figures, then shortly afterwards was seen taking-off again without meeting any opposition at all. Work that one out if you feel like it.

One aspect of the Hess flight that is beyond dispute, however, is the fact (some say coincidental) that on the day he landed in Scotland, the sustained German night bombing campaign against Britain came to a sudden end. Many historians

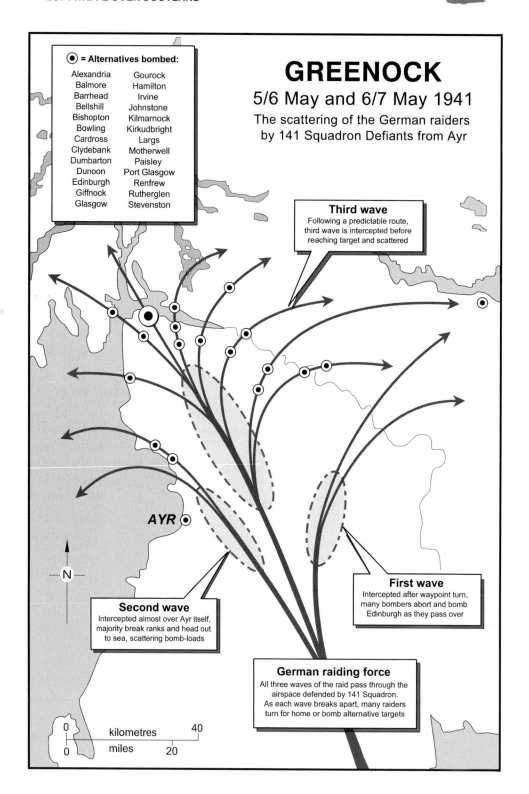

**= Alternatives bombed:**

| | |
|---|---|
| Alexandria | Gourock |
| Balmore | Hamilton |
| Barrhead | Irvine |
| Bellshill | Johnstone |
| Bishopton | Kilmarnock |
| Bowling | Kirkudbright |
| Cardross | Largs |
| Clydebank | Motherwell |
| Dumbarton | Paisley |
| Dunoon | Port Glasgow |
| Edinburgh | Renfrew |
| Giffnock | Rutherglen |
| Glasgow | Stevenston |

# GREENOCK
## 5/6 May and 6/7 May 1941
The scattering of the German raiders
by 141 Squadron Defiants from Ayr

**Third wave**
Following a predictable route, third wave is intercepted before reaching target and scattered

**First wave**
Intercepted after waypoint turn, many bombers abort and bomb Edinburgh as they pass over

**Second wave**
Intercepted almost over Ayr itself, majority break ranks and head out to sea, scattering bomb-loads

**German raiding force**
All three waves of the raid pass through the airspace defended by 141 Squadron. As each wave breaks apart, many raiders turn for home or bomb alternative targets

AYR

N

kilometres 40
miles 20

*The wreckage of Rudolf Hess's Messerschmitt Bf-110 at Floors Farm, Eaglesham after he had parachuted out of the aircraft during the night of 10 May 1941. The fabric-covered control surfaces have been stripped bare by souvenir hunters. The fuselage section can now be seen at the Imperial War Museum in London. (Courtesy Imperial War Museum)*

*Typical of the multi-national make-up of the fighter pilots defending northern Scotland was Sergeant Alois Dvorak of 310 (Czechoslovakian) Squadron, seen here at RAF Dyce in July 1941 with the squadron mascot, a Scottish Terrier named Meetya, in front of Dvorak's Hurricane II. Dvorak was killed on 24 September 1941 while flying from Montrose back to Aberdeen when he flew into Leachie Hill near Stonehaven. (Courtesy Airmen's Association of the Czech Republic)*

have claimed that this was evidence of the real purpose of Hess's mission, which was the brokering of an undeclared cease-fire between Hitler and Churchill in the mutually destructive bombing campaign. If this was indeed the case, then nobody told Luftflotte 5 in Norway, who in the meantime continued their own campaign against northern and eastern Scotland without let-up.

Meanwhile the mighty German battleship *Bismarck* was sent off on a mission out into the Atlantic. A cynic might suggest that if there had been a secret cease-fire deal, then this was a good way of keeping the newspapers occupied during this sudden cessation of bombing hostilities. In a little over a month, they would have far more important events in the east to report than a mere battleship loose in the Atlantic. Aircraft from Wick had found *Bismarck* lurking in a Norwegian fjord on 21 May, while aircraft from Hatston went one better the next day, reporting her gone, and the great 'Sink the *Bismarck*' chase was on.

All through the summer months, the Luftwaffe raids went on all up the east coast. One bomber making a rare expedition to the west coast never came back. The Junkers Ju-88 had flown across to the western Highlands where it attacked the warship HMS *Ethiopian* in Loch Ewe. This anchorage was a strategically vital assembly point for Atlantic convoys and was very heavily defended by both light and heavy AA guns. Consequently, the German crew from KG 30 at Stavanger-Sola paid with their lives for their reckless bravery, but not before half a dozen children playing outside the small Bualnaluib School at Aultbea saw the crew waving at them as the bomber banked overhead before starting its bombing run.

High summer in northern Scotland produced other results. On the night of 25/26 June, a formation of no less than three Heinkel He-111s was confirmed shot down into the North Sea off the Scottish coast. No RAF fighters nor anyone else claimed them. In the half-light of a northern summer night, on a flat-calm sea, anti-aircraft gunners on ships were in a perfect position to take pot-shots at the passing raiders, so it is possible that all three fell to naval gunners who were simply unaware of the success they had achieved.

That balmy summer night attracted other raiders, however, and once again it was Fraserburgh that suffered. At 2.15 a.m. a Ju-88 from KG 30 dropped a couple of big 1,000 kg bombs near the harbour. It is unknown what height the raider flew in at,

*An RAF guard of honour at the funeral of Sergeant Alois Dvorak of 310 (Czechoslovakian) Squadron on 29 September at the Old Dyce Churchyard, near Aberdeen. The bodies of several German aircrews shot down in the Aberdeen area were also buried here during the war. (Courtesy Airmen's Association of the Czech Republic)*

but dropping such large bombs with ready-to-explode fuses would have been lethal to the bomber itself at any height below a couple of thousand feet. It is possible that the Junkers was indeed damaged in the huge blasts of its own bombs when it went down out in the North Sea after radioing a distress call to its base at Stavanger-Sola. Back in Fraserburgh, the enormous destructive power of the bombs destroyed what is now the TSB Bank in Broad Street and buried the then-manager and his family in their home, although they were later rescued. In the wake of the two massive town-centre blasts, two people were killed and seventeen others injured. It was reported that many of the injuries were caused by boulders and other debris thrown up by the explosions falling through the roofs of houses. Stones and boulders were found a quarter of a mile away in College Bounds.

People continued to be killed in small coastal towns. On 12 July yet another Ju-88 from KG 30 made its nocturnal way across the North Sea from Stavanger. This time it attacked Lossiemouth without making any effort to hit the nearby RAF airfield. It dropped its entire load on the town, killing four civilians. That same night, other German night raiders were less fussy about where they dropped their bomb-loads. All across rural Aberdeenshire bombs were reported exploding in the middle of lonely fields. The explanation may be that night raiding offered an excuse to avoid well-defended areas, and that tired German bomber crews, more interested in self-preservation, simply wanted to get rid of their bombs and go home.

This increasing reluctance among German bomber crews to take chances over Scotland was beginning to reveal itself more often, and with good reason. German aircrews were not rotated on regular leave like British aircrews, and the pressure of constant combat operations allied to the steady losses they were suffering over Scotland was starting to take its toll on frayed nerves. They could expect little sympathy from those they continued to attack, however. On 17 July two bombers raided that much-abused target Fraserburgh once again. Incredibly, *both* Ju-88s were shot down over the town by the increasingly effective anti-aircraft gun crews. Both crashed out at sea. One crew was picked up by the fishing boat *Speedwell* some two miles off Cairnbulg. The four airmen, one of them wounded, had been afloat for some time in their yellow dinghy when they finally attracted the fishing boat's attention.

It would have been interesting to have overheard the conversation that took place between the tough fishermen from bomber-tormented Fraserburgh and their unusual catch of the day.

At the end of July, while eastern Scotland continued to fight off the German intruders, security was tight at Oban when President Roosevelt's special advisor, Harry Hopkins, stepped ashore from a US warship. The German invasion of the Soviet Union had commenced on 22 June, so Hopkins boarded RAF Catalina flying boat W8416 of 210 Squadron and set off on the long flight to the Soviet Union for a first meeting with Josef Stalin, via a short stop at Invergordon. Interestingly,

Invergordon almost booked itself a unique place in world history when a possible venue for the 'Big Three' meeting between Churchill, Stalin and Roosevelt was later discussed. Invergordon was seriously proposed by Churchill's team, but was dropped in favour of Tehran simply because Stalin refused to go anywhere that involved him having to fly there, but especially somewhere that involved a long dog-legged flight all the way to Scotland. 'Man of Steel' indeed....

July and August continued to see German raiders operating over the north and east coasts, but the raids were becoming noticeably less frequent, and usually as pointless as ever. On the afternoon of Saturday, 6 August, a Ju-88 bombed and strafed the small Banff distillery at Inverboyndie, setting fire to the buildings. There was a real danger of the stored whisky exploding, and so the entire stock was poured out into the nearby Boyndie Burn. A large turnout of locals then flocked to the scene to witness the unusual sight of extremely inebriated cattle, ducks, seagulls and all other forms of wildlife who had come to appreciate the fine peaty nose of this brand before it all flowed out to sea.

By September, most hit-and-run raids on the east coast of Scotland were now several days apart. Sometimes a full week would pass without a visit from the Luftwaffe. It was not hard to figure out why. The German invasion of the Soviet Union had a direct and profound effect on the lives of people in northern and eastern Scotland. Unlike the rest of Britain, Scotland's tormentors were now exclusively Luftflotte 5 in Norway. At a stroke, this force had to turn around and face an entirely new and potent enemy in northern Russia and Finland. German airfields in Norway were very close to key Soviet bases in Murmansk and Archangel. The Luftwaffe in Norway was about to start suffering losses that would simply dwarf anything they had experienced so far over Scotland. From the late summer of 1941 onwards, the Luftwaffe was transformed from a regular nuisance over Scotland to only an occasional visitor.

But they could still inflict death and destruction when they did appear. Fraser-burgh, of course, continued to be singled-out because of its easy-to-find location. But a raid near a small village south of Aberdeen on 24 September demonstrated the ongoing trait of the Luftwaffe to get their priorities all wrong. The village of Portlethen must have considered itself an unlikely location for a German attack, but it was the Chain Home Low (CHL) radar station at RAF Schoolhill on a hill to the west of the village that was the target. The raiders failed to knock it out, because once again their bombs all failed to explode. Even though the Luftwaffe should have tried to attack this station two years earlier when it might have made a difference, they now refused to give up, and tried again seven days later. Once again, they failed to put the CHL station out of action, and a Ju-88 from KG 30 was shot down in the attempt.

Further up the coast at Peterhead, however, one German bomber had a much better day.

On 29 September, the 'Blue Toon' suffered its worst attack of the war, and it was a single parachute-dropped mine that caused it. These 2 tonne devices erupted in enormous explosions. This particular mine floated down onto James Street, where the huge blast killed people aged from 12 months to 69 years and all ages in between. The damage was spectacular and half the town lost windows, doors or roofs in the tremendous overpressure of the mine's shockwave. Thirty people died.

It was the last big casualty toll inflicted by the Luftwaffe in Scotland in 1941.

One-off raiders still attacked during the rest of the year, but more German bombers were shot down than were Scottish people killed or, for that matter, even injured. The last death of the year inflicted by the Luftwaffe was also near Peterhead, at the local RAF airfield near Longside. On 30 November, a single Ju-88 made a fast and low strafing pass over the airfield, where the Spitfires of 416 Squadron were

*The fighting in the Soviet Union from summer 1941 onwards began to save Scotland from the worst attentions of the Luftwaffe based in Norway. Here, almost a year later, Soviet Foreign Minister Molotov makes his historic arrival at Tealing airfield near Dundee in 1942 en route to meet Churchill in London. (Author's collection)*

based. One pilot was killed and three airmen injured. On 16 December the final raid of the year on Scotland took place, appropriately at Peterhead, where no casualties were sustained.

The hardest year of war in Scotland was over. But the picture had changed dramatically from the same time the year before, when things had looked desperate indeed. Now, not only was the Soviet Union an ally, but the Red Army had finally stopped the German army at the gates of Moscow.

And far across the Atlantic, Uncle Sam was on his way.

APPENDIX 1

# OTHER EVENTS: MARCH TO DECEMBER 1941

**23 March**    Messerschmitt Bf-110 shot down by anti-aircraft fire over Sullom Voe.

**31 March**    Junkers Ju-88 shot down by 43 Squadron Hurricane off Peterhead.

**2 April**    Raid on Cruden Bay.

**7 April**    Raids on Edinburgh, Dunfermline, Greenlaw, Gretna and Stirling.

**8 April**    Raids on Rosyth and Cowdenbeath.

**16 April**    Raids on Sanquhar, Greenock, Dumbarton and North Berwick.

        Focke-Wulf Fw-200 shot down by 252 Squadron Beaufighter off Aberdeen.

**17 April**    Focke-Wulf Fw-200 shot down by anti-aircraft fire off Shetland.

**22 April**    Raid on Peterhead.

**24 April**    Junkers Ju-88 shot down by anti-aircraft fire over Firth of Forth.

**26 April**    Raid on Pitenweem.

**27 April**    Raid on Wick.

**28 April**    Raid on Cruden Bay.

**29 April**    Focke-Wulf Fw-200 shot down by anti-aircraft fire off Shetland.

**7 May**    Junkers Ju-88 shot down by 43 Squadron Hurricane off Tay Estuary.

**16 May**    Raid on Montrose.

**17 May**    Junkers Ju-88 shot down by anti-aircraft fire off Aberdeen.

**27 May**    Raid on Montrose.

**28 May**    Junkers Ju-88 shot down by 43 Squadron Hurricane over Roxburghshire.

        Junkers Ju-88 shot down by 43 Squadron Hurricane over Iona.

| | |
|---|---|
| **30 May** | Raid on Peterhead. |
| **4 June** | Raids on Fraserburgh and Wick. |
| **5/6 June** | Raid on Aberdeen. |
| | Heinkel He-111 shot down by anti-aircraft fire off Aberdeen. |
| **6 June** | Attack on Convoy off Stonehaven, one ship sunk. |
| | Heinkel He-111 shot down by anti-aircraft fire from convoy off Stonehaven. |
| **8 June** | Junkers Ju-88 shot down by 43 Squadron Hurricane off Eyemouth. |
| **12 June** | Junkers Ju-88 shot down by 500 Squadron Blenheim over Loch Ewe. |
| **13 June** | Heinkel He-111 shot down by anti-aircraft fire off Peterhead. |
| **20 June** | Raid on Peterhead. |
| **21 June** | Raid on Fort William. |
| **9 July** | Raid on Aberdeen. |
| **11 July** | Junkers Ju-88 shot down by anti-aircraft fire off Aberdeen. |
| **14 July** | Raid on Montrose. |
| | Junkers Ju-88 shot down by anti-aircraft fire near Montrose. |
| **18 July** | Junkers Ju-88 shot down by 43 Squadron Hurricane off east coast. |
| **19 July** | Heinkel He-111 shot down by anti-aircraft fire off east coast. |
| **21 July** | Raid on Aberdeen. |
| **24 July** | Raids on Aberdeen and Edinburgh. |
| | Junkers Ju-88 shot down by 43 Squadron Hurricane in Firth of Forth. |
| **August** | Raid on Aberdeen. |
| | Junkers Ju-88 shot down by anti-aircraft fire off Aberdeen. |
| **6 August** | Raid on Aberdeen |
| **8 August** | Raid on Aberdeen. |
| **10 August** | Raid on Peterhead. |
| **14 August** | Heinkel He-111 shot down by 43 Squadron Hurricane off Aberdeen. |
| **16 August** | Raids on Banff, Montrose and Innerwick, East Lothian. |

| | |
|---|---|
| **18 August** | Raids on Peterhead and Aberdeen. |
| **5 September** | Raid on Peterhead. |
| **6 September** | Junkers Ju-88 shot down by 43 Squadron Hurricane off east coast. |
| **7 September** | Raid and convoy attack at Fraserburgh. |
| **8 September** | Raid on Peterhead. |
| **13 September** | Two Heinkel He-111s shot down by anti-aircraft fire in Firth of Forth. |
| **3 November** | Raid on Dundee. |
| **14 November** | Raid on Fraserburgh. |
| **15 November** | Raid on Peterhead. |
| **22 November** | Raid on Aberdeen. |
| **23 November** | Raid on Rosyth. Heinkel He-111 shot down by anti-aircraft fire in Firth of Forth. |
| **18 December** | Junkers Ju-88 shot down by anti-aircraft fire off Shetland. |
| **22 December** | Junkers Ju-88 shot down by anti-aircraft fire off Shetland. |
| **29 December** | Junkers Ju-88 shot down by anti-aircraft fire off Shetland. |

# 7

## *1942–1943*

## THE FINAL STING IN THE TAIL

German bombing attacks on Scotland tailed off dramatically in the summer of 1942 and to all appearances seemed to finally come to an end. Unfortunately this would prove to be wishful thinking.

The year began with the standard pattern of hit-and-run raids in the northern and eastern coastal areas of Scotland. One raider selected the tiny village of Newburgh north of Aberdeen as a target. A small jetty was in commercial use here at the mouth of the River Ythan, and it may simply have been an opportunistic target for a raider looking for something quick and easy to bomb so that it could escape back out to sea again. Damage was negligible. Wick received its first visit of the year from the Luftwaffe on 23 January, but this would turn out to be the last bombing raid ever suffered by the town. Peterhead was singled out again the following day. After dropping a parachute mine off neighbouring Boddam, a raider turned for home over the town, strafing the streets below with cannon and machine-gun fire as it made its escape out to sea. Poor little Newburgh was once again attacked by a lone bomber a day later.

The new year began to look as if it would become a repeat performance of the previous year, when another raider made a determined attack on Hellfire Corner three days later. The German aircraft arrived at Peterhead, flew right up Queen Street, strafing all the way, then followed the coast up to Fraserburgh. Here it circled the area, carefully choosing a target then dropped two large bombs on the small fishing

*Spitfire pilots of 'B' Flight of 602 Squadron pose for the camera at RAF Peterhead in 1942. On the right is Flying Officer Julian Marryshow from Trinidad, who in June 1941 volunteered to become one of the RAF's few black fighter pilots.*
*(Courtesy Caribbean Aircrew Association)*

village of Rosehearty. Two houses were hit and completely demolished. Eleven women and children were killed and seven others injured. The raider then turned towards Fraserburgh, no doubt intending to drop the rest of his bomb-load, but was beaten off by a ferocious barrage of anti-aircraft fire from alerted gunners.

Strafing was clearly becoming an increasingly popular pastime in the Luftwaffe. On the first day of February a Junkers Ju-88 made a brave strafing attack on the airfield at RAF Sumburgh, before dashing away in the face of return fire from the airfield defences. The raider damaged some number 404 Squadron Blenheims and riddled a hangar with cannon fire, killing two airmen and injuring six more. It may well be that a similar airfield attack was attempted the following day at RAF Leuchars, but if so the target was missed by a good mile or so. There can be no other reason to explain why Guardbridge in Fife was attacked by this raider, other than the possibility that the anti-aircraft defences around the neighbouring airfield may have been effective enough to persuade the German pilot to get rid of his bombs and flee out to sea.

German aircraft stayed away from Scotland until 14 February, when Fraserburgh was once again attacked. At 7.45 a.m. a single raider circled the town then carefully

*A KG 30 ground crewman poses by the tail of a Junkers Ju-88, proudly displaying where the latest shipping victim has been painted. The tally shows that the aircraft has attacked twelve ships and sunk another four. This may seem optimistic, but in addition to attacking shipping off Scotland's east coast, KG 30 also attacked convoys sailing from Loch Ewe to Murmansk, and so the claims may well be accurate. (Courtesy O.I. Vignes)*

dropped five bombs in a neat row along the beach. These did little more than damage some roof tiles on a beach pavilion 400 yards east of the big toolwork factory, which was probably the target. The people of Fraserburgh were to enjoy from then on the novelty of a full year without another hostile visit from the Luftwaffe. The raids were becoming far less frequent; a fact confirmed when the next raider did not appear until a full two weeks later, this time dropping some bombs near Dunbar before escaping out to sea. On 10 March a single bomb was dropped near Sumburgh airfield. As if to highlight the growing feebleness of these German attacks, an RAF Beaufort then succeeded in causing more damage to Sumburgh airfield than any enemy aircraft ever had. Armed with a torpedo, the 404 Squadron aircraft had swung on landing with engine trouble and crashed into the squadron offices, setting them on fire. The airfield tannoy warned everyone to clear the area before the torpedo exploded, which it duly did, wrecking half the buildings on the airfield with a huge blast.

But still the raiders came in, and still they kept being shot down. Two more went down before March ended and then two more during the first fortnight of April. Interspersed with this steady attrition rate of aircraft over Scotland, the Luftwaffe sometimes hit back in force, and did so on the night of 25 April, when both Peterhead and Aberdeen were attacked. The King Street area of Aberdeen was particularly badly wrecked, with tram-lines and granite cassies ripped up and the road badly cratered. Urquhart Road was also hit and a house at 22 Summerfield Terrace received a direct hit. Two people were killed in the raid and twenty-five injured. Peterhead, as usual, received a fleeting visit with some bombs dropped for no other effect than to awaken the entire town in the middle of the night again. Earlier in the day a 43 Squadron Hurricane had brought down a torpedo-armed Heinkel He-115 just offshore from Aberdeen. The German losses increased when yet another Ju-88 and an He-111 were shot down off the coast.

A small training airfield at Tealing north of Dundee received some unusual visitors on 29 April. Shortly after dawn, a large four-engine bomber with red star markings arrived in the circuit and landed at this otherwise anonymous airfield. This was a Soviet Petlyakov Pe-8 and stepping down from the aircraft to be met by some Government officials was none other than the Soviet Foreign Minister Molotov, dressed in flying gear and woolly boots. He'd flown direct from the Soviet Union in order to meet Churchill at Chequers, and done so in an unheated, unpressurised and uncomfortable bomber at high altitude over hostile German-controlled airspace. The event had proved to be a great advert for the supposedly unreliable Soviet aircraft industry, but the same day proved to be a bad one for the British aircraft industry. Offered the choice of one of two elegant de Havilland Flamingo aircraft to fly south to London in, Molotov made the right choice; the other one crashed in the Vale of York, killing everyone aboard, including most of the top-brass who had met him at Tealing. The airfield had been deliberately chosen as a quiet, out-of-the-way location for a series of high-profile visits that would culminate in the signing of the Anglo-Russian Treaty in London. Little Tealing would never again find itself in such a media spotlight.

In the skies over Scotland, German aircraft were now becoming increasingly scarce. The month of May saw only one *Wekusta* aircraft being encountered and attacked over Scotland. The Heinkel He-111 was shot down by a 125 Squadron

Beaufighter after it had been attacked by a Spitfire from RAF Peterhead, although from then on the *Wekustas* were to be left alone after their radio codes had been cracked and the RAF started listening-in on their useful weather reports. The presence of increasingly modern aircraft operating from a growing number of new airfields in northern Scotland showed how potentially dangerous this airspace was becoming for German aircraft. As if to confirm the fact another Beaufighter, this time a 248 Squadron machine operating from Shetland, shot down a Blohm und Voss Bv-138 flying boat that had pushed its luck too far by approaching Lerwick on 8 June. Three days later two more Junkers Ju-88s were shot down off the east coast, one by the highly effective anti-aircraft defences in the Moray Firth and the other by an equally effective 416 Squadron Spitfire off Peterhead.

July, for the first time in two years, saw a complete absence of bandits in the skies of Scotland.

But if people assumed that this meant they had seen the last of the Luftwaffe they were to be proved wrong on 6 August, when raiders once more swept in fast and low over the east coast. Bombs were dropped in the Craigentinny district of Edinburgh and at St Andrews, where some damage was caused. Considerably more damage resulted on 7 August, when a night attack on Aberdeen caused the last civilian bombing casualties in Scotland of 1942. Several raiders raced in and dropped bomb-loads that fell around the harbour area, hitting South Market Street hardest of all. Several buildings were demolished. A nurse and two members of a rescue squad were killed when a building collapsed while they were searching it for survivors. In all, seven people were killed that night. Five days later the airfield at RAF Drem, which had been involved in the destruction of so many German raiders from the very outset of the war, was finally attacked itself. As if seeking belated retribution a single Ju-88 flew in over the airfield and bombed it, damaging the control tower and four parked Spitfires, but without causing any casualties.

It was the last occasion in 1942 that a bomb was dropped in Scotland. As time went on, people began to believe it might prove to be the last ever raid on Scotland. With every month that went by without another, it looked as if they could be right. On 22 August another Bv-138 flying boat was shot down by a 248 Squadron Beaufighter. Three days later, the Caithness Hills claimed the life of everyone aboard an RAF Sunderland when it flew into Eagle Rock. Sunderlands were crashing or disappearing with terrible regularity while operating from northern Scottish seaplane bases, losing all their crews in the process. On board this particular one happened to be the Duke of Kent, giving what was otherwise just another tragic Sunderland crash a more lasting reason to be remembered – in the eyes of some people at least.

On 16 September number 248 Squadron once more proved that they were the masters of the skies around Shetland when they brought down a KG 26 Heinkel He-111 near Fair Isle. During November, the anti-aircraft defences around the north-east coast would make a similar claim by shooting down two Junkers Ju-88s. To round off the year, 248 Squadron shot down a Ju-88 for Christmas on 25 December.

Luftwaffe bombing attacks were now a rarity in Scotland, and since the summer not a single bomb had been dropped on Scottish soil. There was every reason to believe that no more would be dropped, as the wider picture was now beginning to look decidedly bleak for the Nazi regime in Berlin. The eyes of the world were now fixed on a huge city on the banks of the River Volga deep inside the Soviet Union. Here in Stalingrad, the German Sixth Army was poised on the verge of a catastrophic defeat. Zhukov's awesome pincer movement, covering an area almost the size of Scotland, demonstrated that the Red Army had become an unstoppable force that would suck in everything Germany could throw at it.

*The Spitfire pilots of 'B' Flight of 602 Squadron once again pose for the camera, this time at RAF Sumburgh in Shetland in April 1943. Flying Officer Julian Marryshow from Trinidad now carries a pipe, although judging by his woollen gloves and the fact that the Spitfire Mk V is held down by large boulders tied to the wings, the weather in Shetland that April must have been as windy as always. (Courtesy Caribbean Aircrew Association)*

Surely there was nothing to be gained from attacking Scotland any more? Near the end of February 1943 the emphatic answer was delivered at Hellfire Corner.

On the night of 19/20 February 1943 both Peterhead and Fraserburgh were attacked in what seemed like simply another dose of the usual. On this occasion, however, there was rather more to the attack than met the eye. Two years earlier a couple of Norwegian men had been dropped off the north-east coast by a German U-boat, ostensibly to act as German spies. Almost immediately, though, both gave themselves up and were then 'turned' by the British security services. From a safe house in Aberdeen the pair transmitted false information to their German controllers in Norway, until it was felt that in order for the deception to be maintained, the pair should request money and other supplies to be dropped to them. This was duly arranged to take place on the lonely beach at Rattray Head on that February night. At 2.30 a.m. on the 20th a single German bomber appeared over Rattray and dropped a canister of supplies to the two waiting men. That should have been that, but unfortunately the Germans decided to enhance their part in the deception by turning the operation into an attack on nearby Fraserburgh.

Flying low over the Hexagon, the raider dropped four bombs on the School Street area, causing a great deal of damage. The bombs hit a number of high-occupancy tenement houses and also a few small shops in the area. In all some 15 houses were so badly damaged that they had to be demolished, with 470 other properties damaged as well. At number 59 School Street, 11-year-old Lawrence Kerr was sharing a bed with his brother Louis. The bed was blown out into the front garden with both boys still in it, and although Louis was unharmed, his brother was dead. The fourth bomb destroyed the shops of Bruce the butchers and Smith the bakers. Undeterred, baker Dillon Smith started selling his produce from a makeshift counter on the street outside his ruined shop. Mr Main and his wife had a newsagent's shop on the corner of School Street and Mid Street above which they lived. One bomb blew off the entire gable of the building, and the floor of their bedroom tilted so badly that the couple, still together in bed, slid off the first floor and onto the street below without being harmed. The double-agents asked the Germans not to repeat the process.

Earlier that night, Peterhead benefited from the kind of faulty bomb fuses that had already been seen in Fraserburgh, when two large bombs failed to explode after being dropped by a fast and low German raider. This was a particularly lucky escape for Peterhead since the bombs had been dropped into the crowded town centre, one even falling into the Regal cinema. The other heavy bomb landed in a house in nearby Maiden Street, where it passed into local folklore. On its fast and brutal passage through the house, the big bomb had come down the stairs, ripping off all the stair-edge nosings in the process, before bursting through the front door and eventually coming to rest outside in the street.

Clearly senior officers at the headquarters of Luftflotte 5 in Norway saw every reason to continue sending their bombers out on futile missions over Scotland, even though these Scottish skies were becoming a virtual death-trap for the few German aircraft that ventured into them. As if to emphasise the fact, a series of attempted hit-and-run raids on Scotland on 24 and 25 March by assorted Luftflotte 5 units including KG 30 and KG 26 ended in a mauling for the attackers. Five Junkers Ju-88s and one of the newer Dornier Do-217s were shot down, with many others damaged and chased off out to sea. Some bombs were dropped at Kelty, Barrhead and Glasgow, but no co-ordinated attack was attempted. Everything about the defences of Scotland had improved so much that it seemed as if no raid could have any chance of success. Scotland's airspace throbbed to the sound of modern, hard-hitting British aircraft like the Beaufighter and Mosquito, while the fighter defences now included savage beasts like the RAF's new North American P-51 Mustang. In addition, the radio countermeasure Meacon was distorting German navigation beams and luring raiders into the hills with inevitable results, while the anti-aircraft gun crews were also constantly improving.

And yet despite all of this, the next big raid still managed to be a complete surprise, causing heavy loss of life. On that final air attack on Scotland, on 21 April 1943, not a single German aircraft was shot down. The main target was Aberdeen, and the fate of the city had been decided at the 'Wolf's Lair' in East Prussia as the first response to a demand by Adolf Hitler himself.

The wider context of the war explains Hitler's motivations. Stalingrad had now fallen, showing the world that the tide had turned against the Nazi regime. Nothing would now stop the Soviet steamroller from taking revenge all the way to the streets of Berlin. In the skies above the Thousand-Year Reich, RAF Bomber Command

*Bomb damage in the Cattofield area of Aberdeen after the Luftwaffe's last raid on Scotland on 21 April 1943. Like so many other properties damaged in this widespread raid, this building suffered such extensive structural damage that the neighbouring two-up, two-down block of houses had to be demolished and rebuilt. (Courtesy Aberdeen City Libraries)*

continued a relentless nocturnal devastation of German cities. The Führer raged in impotence. The final straw for Hitler came in the spring of that year, when huge formations of American Eighth Air Force bombers began to appear over Germany as well – and in broad daylight.

Hitler had lost all confidence in Göring and at a special meeting at the Wolf's Lair in March of 1943, he raged at Göring and the inability of the Reichmarshall's Luftwaffe to do the same to British cities as the Allies were doing to German ones. Hitler proved he was becoming increasingly deluded by declaring that he was going to give the Luftwaffe 'a final opportunity to rehabilitate itself by reopening reinforced attacks against England'. He wanted to see Britain bombed – and on the same scale that Germany was being bombed. All efforts of the Luftwaffe, Hitler explained, were to be subordinated to this task. But the disgraced Göring was clearly to play no part in it, when Hitler ordered the appointment of a new Luftwaffe post: *Angriffsführer England* (Attack Leader England).

The man chosen to lead this new air offensive was Generalmajor Dietrich Peltz. Naturally enough, his first operation against England was to take place at Aberdeen. Peltz was under no illusions about his task, however, nor the inevitably short time-span of his likely tenure in the role. He would soon be proved right when his orders were quietly shelved after having achieved no strategic effect of any value. Powerful voices within the Luftwaffe such as Adolf Galland were openly calling for every available German aircraft and aircrew to be diverted back to Germany for the urgent air defence of the Reich. The reason was very simple and the popular phrase of the period summed it up perfectly: Hitler may have created a 'Fortress Europe', but he had forgotten to put a roof on it.

Meanwhile, the city of Aberdeen was to become a sacrificial lamb to Hitler's rages. Peltz realised that the special requirements of his task demanded the use of the best bomber currently in the Luftwaffe inventory – the twin-engine Dornier Do-217. This aircraft was fast and capable of carrying up to four tons of bombs, considerably more than the average Ju-88 or He-111. The best squadron was KG 2, based at Soesterberg in the Netherlands, which had already conducted bombing operations over Britain. Unfortunately, their results had made it obvious (though none of Hitler's sycophantic entourage had the courage to tell him so) that the Do-217s were simply unable to replicate the effects of several hundred Lancaster bombers. Although KG 2 were sent to Stavanger-Sola specifically in order to attack Aberdeen, the result was already a foregone conclusion. The attack would kill many innocent people certainly, but because so few bombers were to take part in the raid (29 of them) and because of the scattered way they would undertake the raid, the results would make not one iota of difference to the war, other than to steel the resolve of most Aberdonians to see Germany comprehensively defeated. All the same, KG 2 was obliged to try, and on the direct orders of the Führer himself.

At Stavanger-Sola, the Dorniers were fuelled to the limit and loaded with 3 tons of high-explosive bombs apiece. In the early evening of 21 April in the lengthening daylight of a northern sky, the formation of 29 aircraft took off from Sola and headed out across the North Sea. In truth, the widely scattered gaggle of aircraft, the last a good half-hour behind the first, could hardly be called a formation. They were simply a bunch of aircraft heading in the same direction. After an hour or so in the air, the intended landfall was made over the Bullers of Buchan to the south of Peterhead. Defences that were rather less alert than they might have been a year or so before, together with the well-known thin area of CHL radar coverage near Peterhead, allowed the first bombers to cross the coast and swing south at high speed towards Aberdeen without being detected. At heights of between 200 and 500 feet, the first elements of the formation made their fast run-in towards the city at 10.30 p.m. as dusk began to fall.

The high speed and low height of the raiders precluded any chance of careful target selection, although the main focus of the attack seemed to settle on the Co-operative dairy at Berryden. This harmless facility was selected in a snap-decision by bomber crews who believed that the prominent water tower at the Berryden dairy was actually a flak tower, and must therefore be defending a building worthy of attacking. Other bombers in the formation simply let loose their loads at the first thing they saw. It was all basically a matter of pot-luck. Some bombs missed their targets; others hit them.

North of the city, an entire stick comprising a mixture of 250 kg and 500 kg bombs stitched a line across the golf course north of the Bridge of Don, although it was likely that the nearby Gordon Army Barracks was the intended target. Another bomber made a better effort of it, dropping its load accurately onto the barracks, where one large bomb crashed into a building, exploded, and killed 27 soldiers inside it.

Meanwhile, the force spread out across Aberdeen as it flew over the city from north to south. A large woollen mill at Grandholme looked a likely target and was attacked, although all the bombs missed. In the northern end of the city, some railway sidings at Kittybrewster were an obvious and highly visible target, and several bombers released their loads here. One entire bomb-load overshot and the bombs formed a line of devastating explosions all the way up nearby Bedford Road, causing huge damage and many casualties.

To the west of the city several bombers seem to have veered inland, some even heading due west. as evidenced by the pattern of the bombs they dropped in the Woodside area. The art-deco school at Middlefield was hit and almost completely destroyed. Nearby houses in Brown Street and in the Cattofield area were devastated by widely scattered bombs – houses not directly hit were instantly reduced to windowless shells by the blasts. Slightly to the south, the huge hospital complex on

Cornhill Road was singled out and several bomb-loads dropped on it. The Royal Mental Hospital at what is now known as Aberdeen Royal Infirmary at Foresterhill was hit and burned out. Damage was widespread all across the hospital grounds with most of the hospital windows being blown in by bomb blasts.

Near the main target of Berryden the bombing was more concentrated, but quickly began to overshoot into the George Street area where large fires broke out. At Causewayend, the front of a church was blown off. All over the city, bombs created incidental damage with blast and shrapnel, killing and injuring people and damaging buildings. Equally as many loads fell into open countryside as hit the city, one even stitching a line of craters on farmland as far west as the village of Kingswells.

For all the logistical effort that had gone into it, the attack was proving to be just another hit-and-run raid, although on a much larger scale than normally seen here in the north-east. One of the German bombers, in a reckless display of murderous intent in the face of the awakening anti-aircraft defences, was watched by thousands of Aberdonians as it circled the city, its 20 mm downward-pointing cannon pumping out shells at anything and everything in its path until its ammunition was exhausted.

Within the space of half an hour, 28 of the bombers had made their individual runs across the city and by 11.05 p.m. were heading back out to sea in the gathering darkness, leaving huge palls of smoke billowing into the sky above Aberdeen. In addition to the 27 soldiers killed at the Gordon Barracks, 98 Aberdonian civilians were dead, most of them women and children. Sunnybank Primary School today displays a plaque in memory of 5 children, all aged under 10, who were killed that night. Ninety-three people were seriously injured and 141 slightly injured. Eight thousand houses were damaged by blast shock-waves and of these 599 were rendered uninhabitable. Fourteen rest centres were opened to accommodate almost 1,000 newly homeless people, while the emergency services struggled to contain 13 major conflagrations in the city.

Further north, the last Dornier to take off from Sola had taken a wrong turn on crossing the coast near Peterhead and flew around northern Aberdeenshire for a while trying to find its bearings. Eventually it found itself flying over Fraserburgh, where it finally jettisoned its load of nine high-explosive bombs plus some incendiaries, before departing for home. These bombs fell just outside Fraserburgh in the Watermill area at Greenbank Croft, at Smiddyhill and North Pitblae. Two people were injured. One, a Mrs McGregor at Greenbank Cottage, had heard a plane fly over and went to the front door to take a look. As she opened it, a bomb exploded nearby and she was hit on the head by a slate falling from her own roof.

These bombs outside Fraserburgh were the last to fall in Scotland in the Second World War and Mrs McGregor's cut to the head was, chronologically speaking, the final Scottish casualty from German bombing.

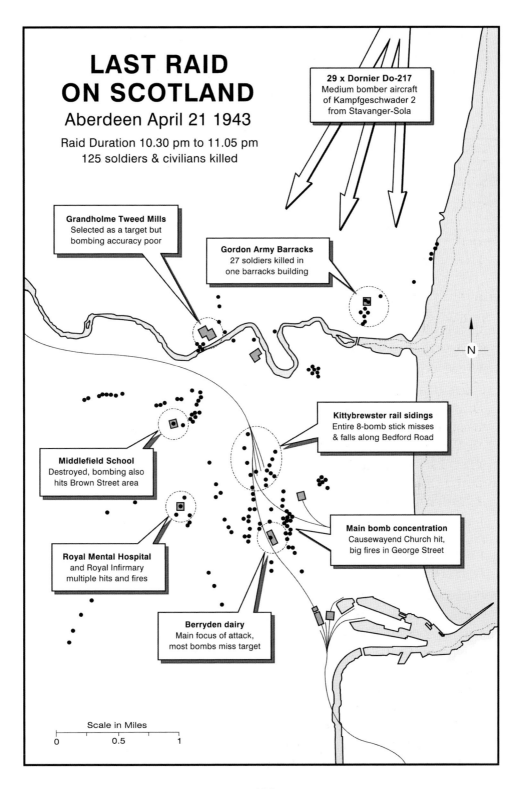

**LAST RAID ON SCOTLAND**

Aberdeen April 21 1943

Raid Duration 10.30 pm to 11.05 pm
125 soldiers & civilians killed

**29 x Dornier Do-217**
Medium bomber aircraft
of Kampfgeschwader 2
from Stavanger-Sola

**Grandholme Tweed Mills**
Selected as a target but
bombing accuracy poor

**Gordon Army Barracks**
27 soldiers killed in
one barracks building

**Kittybrewster rail sidings**
Entire 8-bomb stick misses
& falls along Bedford Road

**Middlefield School**
Destroyed, bombing also
hits Brown Street area

**Main bomb concentration**
Causewayend Church hit,
big fires in George Street

**Royal Mental Hospital**
and Royal Infirmary
multiple hits and fires

**Berryden dairy**
Main focus of attack,
most bombs miss target

N

Scale in Miles

0     0.5     1

## LAST GERMAN BOMBING RAID ON SCOTLAND

Dornier Do-217 E-2 of Kampfgeschwader 2, one of the aircraft
which bombed Aberdeen and Fraserburgh on 21 April 1943

For Hellfire Corner and the rest of the north-east of Scotland, the air attacks were finally over, even though nobody at the time could know that this was the case, especially when another raider headed in over Aberdeenshire from the sea at around 4 p.m. Sunday, 9 May.

The aircraft was yet another Junkers Ju-88, but the difference this time was that the aircraft was a radar-equipped R-1 night-fighter version from 10./NJG 3 in Norway, and that the crew, led by Oberleutnant Heinrich Schmitt, had made up their minds to defect.

Despite the many conspiracy theories that later surrounded the arrival of this aircraft, none was involved. Schmitt and his crew had been ordered to try to intercept the unarmed BOAC Mosquito that made the regular high-speed run between Sweden and RAF Leuchars. For whatever their personal reasons, the crew had unanimously agreed to bring an end to their war by defecting to Scotland and surrendering. All they had to do was survive the attempt. Their aircraft was fitted with the brand-new FuG 202 Lichtenstein BC low-band UHF air interception radar, complete with nose-mounted 'Matratze' aerial array. This radar had been helping German night-fighter crews wreak havoc among Allied bombers in the night skies over Germany, and the British were desperate to get their hands on a set to try to find out how to jam it.

*The Junkers Ju-88 night-fighter that defected to Aberdeen on Sunday, 9 May 1943 with its valuable air-interception radar. The German pilot flew around in circles off the Ythan estuary in order to attract the attention of the local radar controllers, who sent Spitfires off to intercept and escort the Junkers into Dyce.*
*(Author's collection)*

Once out over the North Sea that afternoon, the crew put their plan into action. First, they signalled to their base that they were having engine failure and were going to ditch into the sea. Then they headed for Scotland. Approaching Peterhead they turned south, and at a height that made them clearly visible to the radar operators at Hillhead, began circling. The crew knew that this would be obvious to the radar controllers and hoped for the best. At the new Sector Control room at Peterhead, a sharp-eyed controller named Flight Lieutenant G.S. Crimp did indeed notice the unusual behaviour. He ordered Blue section of 165 (Ceylon) Squadron, normally based at Peterhead, but for now detached at Dyce, into the air to intercept, but wisely warned them to hold their fire until they could find out what was going on. Two Mark VB Spitfires soon made visual contact off the coast near the Ythan estuary. On seeing them, the Junkers immediately started firing off flares, waggled its wings and then lowered its undercarriage – the signal that denoted an aircraft's intention to surrender. Spitfire Blue One waggled its wings in return then took up position ahead of the German aircraft to lead it into Dyce. Blue Two stayed behind and above the German aircraft, ready to fire if the bandit tried anything untoward. In line astern, the three aircraft came in and landed at Dyce, where the Junkers was quickly recognised for the prize that it was and locked safely away in a hangar under armed guard. Later, it was flown south, where the secrets of its radar were revealed.

Two months later it was back to business as usual off Shetland. A Canadian Beaufighter pilot named 'Slippery' Sid Shulemson of 404 Squadron shot down a Blohm und Voss Bv-138 on 8 July, while the Royal Navy in the form of an 801 Squadron Martlet shot down a Junkers Ju-88 nearby. Nearly three weeks later on the 28th Shulemson was at it again, this time flying from Wick with the rest of his squadron. Encountering a formation of more Bv-138s making a suicidal approach to Shetland, Shulemson and his 404 Squadron comrades shot down four of them in quick succession, and were only prevented from making it five when another Fleet Air Arm Martlet from HMS *Illustrious* raced in and shot down the last one. Three of the German crewmen, Leutnant Knittel, Unteroffizier Hengst and Unteroffizier Mohlau, were later rescued by a U-boat. A week later these three men were still aboard the U-boat when it was sunk by more RAF aircraft. Once again, all three men were rescued from the sea, but this time their rescuers were the crew of a British warship and all three finally found themselves in captivity.

Before the year was over nine more German aircraft would be shot down off the Scottish coasts, mostly in the Shetland area, where no German aircraft could now operate without being attacked. On 22 November the Polish number 307 night-fighter squadron, equipped with Mosquitoes, were on temporary 'rest' at Sumburgh, when they intercepted and shot down a very rare bird, one of the first Heinkel He-177 *Greif* bombers to see operational service.

*The first of two photographs showing the destruction of a Blohm und Voss Bv-138 flying boat off the east coast of Scotland. The German aircraft was shot down off Shetland on 8 July 1943 by a Canadian 404 (Buffalo) Squadron Beaufighter from Wick, flown by Flight Lieutenant Sidney Shulemson. The three-engine aircraft has been hit by cannon fire in the central engine and is well on fire, heading for the sea. (Courtesy T. Coughlin)*

*The second picture in the sequence shows the Bv-138 after hitting the water as seen from Shulemson's Beaufighter. The fire that has burned away the tail surfaces is out, but the aircraft is already sinking due to cannon-fire damage. Although the rubber liferaft has automatically deployed, the Luftwaffe crew, possibly trapped or wounded inside the aircraft, were all killed. Twenty days later, 404 Squadron would shoot down another five of these flying boats in the same area, all on the same day. (Courtesy T. Coughlin)*

As 1943 ended it was clear that something very unusual was going on out in the Moray Firth, which seemed to be filled to the horizon with every type of ship imaginable. On the isolated beaches of the Culbin Sands, a massive Allied invasion exercise was taking place.

The sight of thousands of troops wading ashore seemed to bode well for 1944.

*Germany's belated attempt to build a heavy four-engine bomber was not a success. The Heinkel He-177 Greif (Griffon) had four engines coupled in pairs to drive two airscrews through a common shaft. The engines were notorious for overheating and catching fire. The aircraft could in theory carry a 5 tonne bomb-load but rarely did. One such He-177 ventured near Shetland on 22 November 1943, and was shot down by the Polish 307 Squadron flying radar-equipped night-fighter Mosquitoes on detachment at Sumburgh.*
*(Courtesy O.I. Vignes)*

# 8

## *1944–1945*

## THE LAST FLIGHT OF THE LUFTWAFFE

Although the bombing of Scotland ended with that twilight attack on the north-east in April 1943, people in Scotland understandably feared that there may be further raids and that they could not afford to drop their guard. As long as there was still a war on, hostile aircraft in Scottish airspace had to be intercepted and shot down whenever possible. By 1944 Britain was one vast aircraft carrier and the skies of northern and eastern Scotland were constantly alive with the sound of aero-engines. Aircraft could be seen and heard everywhere, every day. Never before had the skies been so crowded, nor so carefully watched.

Perhaps that's why the crew of Mosquito DZ557 saw what they claimed they saw in broad daylight on 2 January 1944. Having taken off from RAF Dyce in mid-morning, Warrant Officer Able and his navigator headed down the east coast on a routine patrol. Both men claimed that at 12 noon, at 22,000 feet off Alnwick, they saw four large black rectangular objects stationary in the sky ahead of them. Their report was considered serious enough to be forwarded to 13 Group Headquarters, where it was received with interest and then archived, never to be heard of again. Interestingly, a wartime RAF radar specialist named Arthur C. Clark would later make his fortune writing about similar black rectangular objects.

A more standard interception was made on 22 February by the Spitfires of 602 Squadron, now in residence at Sumburgh in Shetland. A vapour trail was spotted at 32,000 feet and the bandit chased by two Spitfires, who caught up with what turned out to be a long-range Bf-109 fighter belonging to the recce unit 1.(F)/120 from Sola. It was quickly shot down into the sea. One of the 602 Squadron pilots based here at this time was the charismatic figure of Flight Sergeant Julian Marryshow, one of the few black pilots in RAF Fighter Command. There is surely some satisfaction in the knowledge that a member of the 'master race' might have been shot down by an Afro-Caribbean pilot like Marryshow.

Meanwhile various types of Junkers bombers from Norway kept trying their luck over Scotland. On 5 March a Ju-88 made the rash move of flying over Lerwick at 600 feet and was shot down by the AA defences for its trouble. On 22 April a Ju-188 was shot down by two Spitfires from 504 Squadron at Castletown on a dusk patrol. Two more recce Ju-188s got away with it when one flew over Wick at 'zero feet' on 18 May, while another did the same over Inverness on the 21st. These twin-engine aircraft were by now taking a desperate gamble over Scotland, and yet another one was spotted and attacked without hesitation on 11 June by two Spitfires from number 118 Squadron. Unfortunately, their aircraft recognition skills were not up to those of the Observer Corps, and the Spitfires had shot down an RAF Mosquito of Coastal Command. The Mosquito Mk VI of 333 (Norwegian) Squadron was based at Wick and was on transit to Shetland when attacked. The navigator, Lieutenant Odd Gjestrum, was killed. Later in the month another Junkers Ju-188 from 1.(F)/120 made the fatal error of flying into the Highlands in the dark. It did not get very far before it flew into a hill near Rothes, killing all its crew.

The summer months of 1944 saw almost no enemy air activity over Scotland, there being matters of greater importance now taking place on the coast of Normandy to occupy much of the Luftwaffe resources. On 25 October the crew of a Ju-52 seaplane decided they had also seen enough of the war and decided to defect. Taking no chances, they put their floatplane down onto the sea some 30 miles east of Aberdeen and waited for the next passing fishing boat to pick them up. It was an optimistic move, but it paid off when both men were rescued and taken prisoner.

By autumn, a major new force had been created in Scotland in the shape of the Banff and Dallachy Strike Wings. Tasked with attacking enemy shipping and U-boats in Scandinavian waters, the presence of these ferociously powerful wings now made a venture into Scottish airspace seem like an impossible proposition for enemy aircraft. Other long-standing problems were now also being dealt with. From Lossiemouth and Milltown, and on one occasion from Banff, the heavily modified Lancasters of numbers 9 and 617 (the Dambusters) squadrons launched attacks on the German battleship *Tirpitz*, finally sinking her on 12 November in Tromso Fjord with their massive 'Tallboy' bombs. Several witnesses claim that one of the Tallboys actually fell off a Lancaster taxiing along the perimeter track at Banff and that the airfield had to be cleared of all personnel until the bomb was defused. Another tells of the racket when these bombers took off in the middle of the night directly over

*A rare photograph of a Lancaster B1 Special, which were modified to carry the enormous 12,000 lb 'Tallboy' bombs used to sink the German battleship* Tirpitz *in Tromsϕ Fjord on 12 November 1944. The force of Lancasters from 617 and 9 Squadrons used a variety of airfields on the north-east coast, including Lossiemouth, Milltown, Dallachy and Banff. This aircraft is pictured at Lossiemouth after the raid. (Author's collection)*

nearby Portsoy. Had yet another Tallboy fallen off a Lancaster at that point, there would have been very little left of Portsoy to talk about.

The pilot of a single engine Bf-109 fighter made the brave decision to fly across the North Sea and land directly at RAF Dyce in order to defect on 26 December, although he ground-looped and wrecked his aircraft on landing. To round off the year in traditional style, two more Junkers fell over Scotland on 29 December. Both were Ju-188s, with the first coming down in Loch Broom on the west coast. The second, however, posed rather more of a worry for Scapa Flow, where it was shot down by aircraft from 611 squadron. This aircraft was photographing warships in preparation for a *Mistel* strike that was being planned for the naval anchorage. The *Mistel* was one of the increasingly desperate weapons then being used by the Luftwaffe. It involved mounting a fighter aircraft on a frame attached to a larger aircraft like a Ju-88 that was unmanned and packed to the seams with high-explosives. The fighter pilot flew the combination directly at the target and then released the bigger aircraft at it before escaping in the smaller fighter. The explosions caused by the *Mistels* were huge and indiscriminate and would have caused much devastation at Scapa Flow, both onshore as well as offshore, had the operation not been cancelled.

The last Christmas of wartime was celebrated with abandon on airfields all over northern Scotland, where the threat of meeting death at the hands of the Luftwaffe was still very real as long as the state of war still persisted. At that point it began to look as if the war would continue for a long time yet, when the supposedly beaten German army mounted an unexpected new offensive in the forest of the Ardennes.

The new year saw even less Luftwaffe activity over Scotland than ever before. A solitary Ju-188 was shot down off the east coast on 4 January 1945. On 20 March a short hit-and-run raid in southern England became known as the very last operation over Britain by the Luftwaffe. All the same, three weeks after this a Luftwaffe Arado Ar-234 *Blitz* jet bomber made a number of armed high-speed flights over Scotland, with the last one taking place on 10 April. The jet flew from Scapa Flow down to the Tay estuary without being intercepted. These were recce flights intended to check Allied shipping concentrations, since the Germans were convinced that an invasion of Norway was imminent.

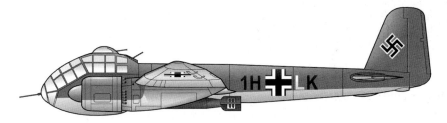

## LAST FLIGHT OF THE LUFTWAFFE

Junkers Ju-188 of Lufttorpedostaffeln 3/KG26, one of the aircraft that took part in the very last Luftwaffe air attack of the war on 21 April 1945, which was intercepted by Banff Strike wing

Four days later what must have been one of the most bizarre U-boat sinkings in history took place off Boddam, near Peterhead. There are many confirmed reports of what happened to *U-1206* that day.

The U-boat was a late-model type VIIC, equipped with a *Schnorkel* device to allow it to stay submerged for longer periods. This, however, meant that the practice of venting the interior of the boat for fresh air, and also of discharging sewage from the toilets, could not take place as often as in a normal U-boat, although it was the latter of the two problems that caused the most discomfort for the submarine crews. Consequently, an innovative new flushing toilet was designed and installed aboard *U-1206*. This toilet, which flushed waste directly out into the sea, was naturally very dangerous to use while the boat was submerged, requiring a sequence of valves to be opened and closed in the correct order to prevent seawater coming into the boat instead of sewage going out. So complex was the procedure that a technician was

*An Arado Ar-234 Blitz jet bomber of the type that flew over Scotland on 10 April 1945. The high-speed flight this small twin-engine aircraft made down the east coast, from Scapa Flow to the Firth of Forth, was the last combat mission flown by a Luftwaffe aircraft directly over Britain during the Second World War. (Courtesy O.I. Vignes)*

specially trained to undertake this task among his other duties. Naturally, he was known by the rest of the crew as the 'Shit Man' even though his job was vital to the safety of the boat and its crew.

The captain of *U-1206*, Captain Karl Adolf Schlitt (an unfortunate surname in the circumstances), however, was a vain man and while en route to the boat's patrol area in the Moray Firth, decided to flush the toilet himself while the boat was rounding the north-east coast at Peterhead. Inevitably, the captain got the sequence wrong and seawater began to flood into the boat, but especially into the battery compartment where deadly chlorine gas began to fill the hull. The boat was forced to surface and because there was a fault with the diesel engines, was unable to move. When British aircraft and armed trawlers in the vicinity began to approach the U-boat, the captain decided to scuttle her and she quickly sank. The crew eventually paddled ashore in their rubber dinghies, although three men were killed on the rocks at Boddam trying to scramble ashore in the heavy seas.

If the idea of sending a U-boat out on patrol in hostile Scottish waters at this late stage of the war seemed like a pointless one, then the notion of mounting an air attack against Scotland a week afterwards can only be described as a suicidally futile one. Nonetheless Scotland's old foes in the shape of KG 26 – now equipped with Junkers Ju-88 and Ju-188 torpedo bombers, were somehow given just such an impossible task in these last few weeks of the war. It should be noted that although the Luftwaffe in continental Europe had by this time been effectively wiped out and no longer constituted an effective force; the Luftwaffe in Norway, by contrast, was still a large and powerful force, well equipped with the latest German aircraft and well stocked with ammunition and fuel. It was the last bastion of military strength of the Nazi regime, and somebody in that regime decided to use it, no matter how pointless the effort. The operation took place on 21 April and was the last attack ever mounted by the Luftwaffe during the Second World War.

Quite who issued the ludicrous order for the raid is unclear. It was certainly not Göring himself, because on the morning the operation took place, the Reichsmarshall and his entourage were fleeing by road from Berlin towards the relative safety of Berchtesgaden. The blame must therefore be laid at the feet of the commanding general of the Luftwaffe in Norway at that time, Generalleutnant Ernst-August Roth. This six-foot-two man was supposedly an evangelical Christian, but his actions reveal the mentality of a fanatical Nazi unable to accept the inevitability of impending defeat. Nothing could possibly be gained by attacking Scotland at that point in time, but still the attack went ahead.

Eighteen aircraft from Lufttorpedostaffeln 2 and 3 of KG 26 took off from Stavanger-Sola that day. Their mission was officially classed as an armed reconnaissance sweep of the north-east Scottish coast. Based on their previous track-record, this would indicate that the formation intended to look for targets of opportunity among merchant shipping off the Rattray Head and Kinnaird Head areas. Each Junkers carried a large torpedo under each wing, inboard of the engines. This was to be a major anti-shipping strike.

As luck would have it, an even larger force of twin-engine strike aircraft, 42 Mosquitoes from Banff Strike Wing, were in the air over the North Sea at exactly the same time as KG 26 were. Their escort of P-51 Mustangs from Peterhead had been given permission to race for home as a big party was scheduled at their base for that night. But the Mosquitoes needed no escort to deal with KG 26 when they found them at a height of only 600 feet in rain and poor visibility. The result was a foregone conclusion. The fight was short, sharp and brutal. The Mosquitoes were normally armed with four 20 mm cannon in their bellies and four machine guns in the nose. Some of them were upgraded versions known as 'Tsetses', with a huge 57 mm anti-tank gun (designed to puncture U-boat hulls) in place of the 20 mm cannons. The most remarkable aspect of the encounter is that any German aircraft survived at all. Precisely how many German aircraft were shot down has always been a matter of some debate.

Initially, Banff Strike Wing aircrews claimed that they had shot down nine of the raiders, with several more 'probables' for no loss to themselves. After the war the commander of the Mosquito formation, Wing-Commander Foxley-Norris, described in his autobiography of meeting a former senior Luftwaffe officer based in Norway during the war, who assured him that only two aircraft made it back to crash-land at Stavanger-Sola that day. Since then, it has become clear that two others crash-landed at other Norwegian bases. One further 'kill' by a Mosquito of 333 (Norwegian) Squadron from Banff was later confirmed, bringing the total confirmed kills to ten German aircraft. This leaves four further aircraft that were never accounted for nor

*North American P-51 Mustang III fighters of 19 Squadron based at RAF Peterhead from the end of 1944 until the end of the war. These were primarily engaged in long-range escort missions to Norway with the strike wings based at Banff and Dallachy, although they were also a formidable air defence presence over Scotland late in the war. (Author's collection)*

seen again, providing a total 'kill' tally for the day of fourteen German aircraft shot down.

The last Luftwaffe mission of the Second World War had ended in a disaster for them, and although the crews of the Mosquitoes who landed back at Banff that day could not know it, they had in fact taken part in the last air battle ever to have been fought in the skies of northern Europe.

Like the story of James Isbister in Orkney in 1940, a story now airbrushed out of most history books, these facts are worth emphasising because they too are often overlooked or deliberately ignored. For example, in 1997 a book entitled *The Last Flight of the Luftwaffe* devoted its entire narrative to the premise that a Luftwaffe fighter attack on American bombers over Germany on 7 April 1945 was the final operation, indeed, the final *flight*, of the Luftwaffe in the Second World War. And yet it was one that took place a full two weeks *before* the air battle between KG 26 and Banff Strike Wing off the Scottish east coast.

The eyes of the world may have been on Scotland at the start of the war, when all the 'firsts' were taking place, but they were no longer looking by the end of it, when many of the 'lasts' were still being played out far away from the photogenic ruins of Germany itself. And there were more to come.

At 5.20 p.m. on 30 April Britain's last air-raid warning siren sounded simultaneously over Aberdeen and Montrose. Some two hours earlier, Hitler had shot himself in Berlin.

*RAF over Scotland. A seventeen-ship formation of Mosquitoes, a small part of the six-squadron Banff Strike Wing, fly over the tower at RAF Banff prior to setting out for another mission over Norway in early 1945. In the last weeks of war, the wing fought the last air battle ever to take place in the skies of northern Europe when they met a formation of German Junkers torpedo bombers off the north-east coast of Scotland and virtually wiped them out. (Author's collection)*

Among the Banff aircraft involved in the battle with KG 26 torpedo bombers on 21 April 1945 were a number of specially modified Mosquitoes known as 'Tsetse' Mosquitoes. This image shows a corporal at RAF Banff demonstrating the bigger bite of these aircraft, in the form of a single 57 mm quick-firing Molins anti-tank gun mounted in place of the standard four cannon in the belly. (Courtesy Chaz Bowyer)

*This dramatic photograph, although not of the highest quality, is remarkable in that it records the instant a Junkers Ju-188 torpedo bomber exploded on being shot down into the sea during the air battle with Banff Strike Wing Mosquitoes on 21 April 1945. (Courtesy Chaz Bowyer)*

On 2 May a Junkers Ju-188 from the ninth *Staffel* of KG 26, the same group so recently mauled by Banff Strike Wing, flew at very low level across the North Sea from Trondheim towards Hellfire Corner. By some miracle it made it without being intercepted or shot down, but instead of looking for targets to attack it came straight in from the sea and landed at RAF Fraserburgh before anyone could do anything about it. There were five crewmen aboard, and all wanted to defect before they were sent out on yet another suicide mission to the dangerous skies over Scotland.

It was the last German aircraft to appear over Britain in the Second World War, but if the fears of its crew seemed exaggerated there was soon evidence that some German commanders cared nothing about the impending end of the war, nor of wasting lives needlessly.

On the very last day of the war, 7 May 1945, newspapers announced the unconditional surrender of German forces and that the following day was to be VE (Victory in Europe) Day. By evening an outpouring of joy filled the night air as people celebrated across the country. For many others it was a moment of intense personal sorrow as those who had not made it this far were quietly remembered.

In Edinburgh huge crowds began dancing eightsome reels at the foot of the Mound to the strains of an Army pipe band. Children gleefully made a mockery of the blackout regulations by lighting bonfires that lit up the skies all along the coast of the Firth of Forth. Out in the Forth, sailors on the 2,878 ton merchant ship SS *Avondale Park*, which had just left Methil, could clearly see the glow of the fires and quietly wished they could have been ashore to join in the celebrations. But at least they were now safe from attack at sea. Three days earlier Hitler's successor, Grand Admiral Dönitz, had ordered that all German U-boats should immediately cease offensive action and surrender to Allied forces.

At 10.40 p.m. the same night near the Isle of May, only some thirty miles from the centre of Edinburgh, where the arrival of peace was being celebrated with such abandon, Kapitänleutnant Emil Klusmeier, commander of the German submarine U-2336, torpedoed the *Avondale Park* and the 1,791 ton Norwegian merchant ship *Sneland I*, sinking both of them within sight of the shore. Two men died on the *Avondale Park* and seven on the *Sneland*. Many people building celebration bonfires on the coasts of Fife and in East Lothian heard the explosions and saw the flames.

Even after so many years of war, people were horrified by such heartless cruelty. Klusmeier refused to acknowledge Dönitz's surrender order, claiming later that he thought it was an Allied ruse and for a few days remained at large out in the North Sea as a potentially hostile renegade. He finally surrendered by sailing his U-boat into Dundee Harbour on 14 May 1945. He never felt the urge to apologise for needlessly killing innocent civilians.

After all nobody else had, and nobody else ever would.

*Appendix A*

## ALL RAIDS ON SCOTLAND
## – TIMELINE FROM 1939 TO 1945

**16 October 1939**
Firth of Forth

**17 October 1939**
Scapa Flow

**13 November 1939**
Sullom Voe

**22 November 1939**
Lerwick

**16 March 1940**
Scapa Flow

**2 April 1940**
Scapa Flow

**8 April 1940**
Scapa Flow

**9 April 1940**
Scapa Flow

**10 April 1940**
Scapa Flow

**25/26 June 1940**
Broxburn

Edinburgh

**26/27 June 1940**
Aberdeen

**29 June 1940**
Peterhead

**30 June**
Aberdeen

**1 July 1940**
Haddington
Wick

**4 July 1940**
Peterhead

**10 July 1940**
Tobermory

**12 July 1940**
Aberdeen
Auchterless
Cupar
Dunfermline
Helensburgh

**13 July 1940**

Stirling
Greenock
Gourock
Dundee

**16 July 1940**
Peterhead
Fraserburgh
Portsoy

**17 July 1940**
Auchtermuchty
Ardeer

**18 July 1940**
Leith
Burntisland
Crail
Edinburgh
Montrose

**19 July 1940**
Glasgow

**20 July 1940**
Ardeer
Stirling
Peterhead
Moffat

**22 July 1940**
Edinburgh
Banff

**23 July 1940**
Montrose
Edinburgh

**24 July 1940**
Hillington
Fife
Aberdeenshire
Glasgow

**26 July 1940**
Kilmarnock

**27 July 1940**
Peterhead
Fraserburgh
Rosehearty
RAF Dyce
Elie, Fife
Kinglassie
Falkland
N. Berwick

**28 July 1940**
Edinburgh
Perth
Glenkindie

**29 July 1940**
Midlothian
Berwickshire

**1 August 1940**
Montrose
Dundee
Haddington
Armadale
Duns

**2 August 1940**
Dundee

**4 August 1940**
Edinburgh

**8 August 1940**
Gourock

**13 August 1940**
Aberdeen
Peterhead
Fraserburgh
St Fergus

**15 August 1940**
Banffshire
Kincardineshire
Montrose

**15 August 1940**
Montrose
Cullen

**18 August 1940**
Montrose

**20 August 1940**
Edinburgh
Glasgow

**21 August 1940**
Hatston, Orkney

**22 August 1940**
Peterhead

**23 August 1940**
Peterhead

**25 August 1940**
Montrose
Invergordon

**27 August 1940**
Aberdeenshire
RAF Edzell
RAF Montrose

RAF Dyce

**28 August 1940**
Monifieth
Aberdeen
Peterhead
Fraserburgh

**30 August 1940**
Dunfermline

**3 September 1940**
Firth of Forth

**4 September 1940**
East Lothian

**17 September 1940**
Glasgow

**18 September 1940**
Glasgow
Rutherglen

**19 September 1940**
Glasgow

**24 September 1940**
Oban

**25 September 1940**
Dundee

**27 September 1940**
Edinburgh

**29 September 1940**
Aberdeen
Fraserburgh
Edinburgh

**2 October 1940**
Bishopton
Montrose
Peterhead

Fraserburgh

**4 October 1940**
Eyemouth
Dunbar

**7 October 1940**
Montrose
Firth of Forth

**8th October 1940**
Edinburgh

**14 October 1940**
Renfrew

**16 October 1940**
Port Glasgow
Arbroath
Kirkwall

**18 October 1940**
Crail
Null Head

**24 October 1940**
Gourock
Glasgow
Johnstone

**24 October 1940**
Gourock

**25 October 1940**
Greenock
Anstruther
St Andrews
RAF Arbroath
Montrose

**26 October 1940**
Ayr
Wick
Cumbernauld
RAF Lossiemouth

**31 October 1940**
Aberdeen

**3 November 1940**
N. Berwick
Bucksburn
Newburgh
Fraserburgh

**4 November 1940**
Aberdeen
Glasgow
Dunfermline
Edinburgh
Kelty
Dundee
Rutherglen
Coatbridge
Larbert

**5 November 1940**
Fraserburgh
Dundee
Aberdeen

**6 November 1940**
Campbeltown

**13 November 1940**
Cumbernauld

**27 November 1940**
E. Linton

**29 November 1940**
Kirkconnel

**20 December 1940**
Glasgow

**21 December 1940**
Glasgow

**22 December 1940**
Fort William

**5 February 1941**
Aberdeen

**7 February 1941**
Fraserburgh

**9 February 1941**
Campbeltown

**13 February 1941**
Aberdeen
Foyers, Inverness

**14 February 1941**
Rosehearty

**15 February 1941**
Invergordon

**17 February 1941**
Lerwick
Invergordon

**19 February 1941**
Portknockie
Fraserburgh
Montrose

**22 February 1941**
Portsoy

**1 March 1941**
Banff

**2 March 1941**
Lerwick

**3 March 1941**
Haddington

**7 March 1941**
Peterhead

**8 March 1941**
Crail

**13/14 March 1941**
Bonnybridge
Clydebank

**14/15 March 1941**
Edinburgh
Clydebank

**16 March 1941**
Fraserburgh

**17 March 1941**
Wick

**19 March 1941**
Rosehearty

**2 April 1941**
Cruden Bay

**4 April 1941**
Fraserburgh

**5 April 1941**
Fraserburgh

**7 April 1941**
Edinburgh
Dunfermline
Greenlaw
Gretna
Stirling

**7/8 April 1941**
Rosyth
Cowdenbeath
Clydebank
Paisley
Cardross
Cumbernauld
Motherwell
Wishaw
Dumbarton
Bishopton
Renfrew
Johnstone

Bonhill
Thurso
Coldstream

**16 April 1941**
Sanquhar
Greenock
Dumbarton
N. Berwick

**17 April 1941**
Fraserburgh

**20 April 1941**
Fraserburgh
Aberdeen

**22 April 1941**
Peterhead

**26 April 1941**
Pittenweem

**27 April 1941**
Wick

**28 April 1941**
Cruden Bay

**5/6 May 1941**
Greenock

**6/7 May 1941**
Greenock

**16 May 1941**
Montrose

**27 May 1941**
Montrose

**28/29 May 1941**
Fort William

**30 May 1941**
Peterhead

**4 June 1941**
Wick
Fraserburgh

**5/6 June 1941**
Aberdeen

**7 June 1941**
Loch Ewe

**12 June 1941**
Loch Ewe

**20 June 1941**
Peterhead

**21 June 1941**
Fort William

**26 June 1941**
Fraserburgh

**9 July 1941**
Aberdeen

**12 July 1941**
Lossiemouth
Aberdeenshire

**14 July 1941**
Montrose

**17 July 1941**
Fraserburgh

**21 July 1941**
Aberdeen

**24 July 1941**
Aberdeen
Edinburgh

**2 August 1941**
Aberdeen

**6 August 1941**
Aberdeen
Banff

**8 August 1941**
Aberdeen
RAF Dyce

**10 August 1941**
Peterhead

**16 August 1941**
Banff
Innerwick
Montrose

**18 August 1941**
Peterhead
Aberdeen

**5 September 1941**
Peterhead

**7th September 1941**
Fraserburgh

**8/9 September 1941**
Peterhead

**11 September 1941**
Aberdeen

**24 September 1941**
Portlethen

**29 September 1941**
Peterhead
Portlethen

**4 October 1941**
Peterhead

**2/3 November 1941**
Dundee

**14 November 1941**
Fraserburgh

**15 November 1941**
Peterhead

**22 November 1941**
Aberdeen

**23 November 1941**
Firth of Forth

**30 November 1941**
RAF Peterhead

**16 December 1941**
Peterhead

**4 January 1942**
Shetland

**12 January 1942**
Newburgh

**23 January 1942**
Wick

**24 January 1942**
Boddam, Peterhead

**26 January 1942**
Newburgh

**29/30 January 1942**
Peterhead

**30 January 1942**
Rosehearty

**31 January 1942**
Eyemouth

**2 February 1942**
Guardbridge

**14 February 1942**
Fraserburgh

**2/3 March 1942**
Dunbar

**10 March 1942**
Sumburgh

**25 April 1942**
Aberdeen
Peterhead

**6 August 1942**
St Andrews
Edinburgh

**7 August 1942**
Aberdeen

**12 August 1942**
RAF Drem

**19/20 February 1943**
Fraserburgh
Peterhead

**25 March 1943**
Edinburgh
Kelty, Fife
Barrhead
Glasgow

**21 April 1943**
Fraserburgh
Peterhead
Aberdeen

# *Appendix B*

## CIVILIAN BOMBING CASUALTIES IN SCOTLAND
## 1939—1945

### North-eastern district

Aberdeen City and counties of Aberdeen, Banff, Kincardine, Moray, Orkney and Shetland

1,243 bombs or parachute mines dropped.

| Killed | Injured and detained in hospital | Slightly injured |
| --- | --- | --- |
| 329 | 270 | 695 |

### Northern district

Inverness and counties of Inverness, Caithness, Nairn, Ross and Cromarty, and Sutherland

222 bombs or parachute mines dropped.

| Killed | Injured and detained in hospital | Slightly injured |
| --- | --- | --- |
| 21 | 9 | 38 |

## South-eastern district

Edinburgh and counties of Midlothian, West Lothian, East Lothian, Roxburgh, Selkirk, Peebles and Berwick

651 bombs or parachute mines dropped.

| Killed | Injured and detained in hospital | Slightly injured |
|---|---|---|
| 27 | 59 | 190 |

## Eastern district

Dundee, and counties of Angus, Fife, Perth and Kinross

779 bombs or parachute mines dropped.

| Killed | Injured and detained in hospital | Slightly injured |
|---|---|---|
| 31 | 37 | 57 |

## Western district

Glasgow, and counties of Argyll, Ayr, Bute, Clackmannan, Dumfries, Dunbarton, Kirkudbright, Lanark, Renfrew, Stirling and Wigtown

3,814 bombs or parachute mines dropped.

| Killed | Injured and detained in hospital | Slightly injured |
|---|---|---|
| 2,112 | 1,792 | 2,578 |

## Summary

Total number of bombs or mines dropped, excluding incendiary containers and isolated rural drops.

| | |
|---|---|
| Killed: | 2,520 |
| Injured and detained in hospital: | 2,167 |
| Slightly injured: | 3,558 |
| **Total casualties:** | **8,245** |

# Appendix C
## GERMAN AIRCRAFT LOSSES OVER SCOTLAND
## 1939—1945

| Date | Type | Location | Unit / Code | Crew / Captain | Details |
|------|------|----------|-------------|----------------|---------|
| 26-9-39 | Dornier Do-18 | North Sea | Küstenstaffel 2./KüFlGr 506 KY+YK | Unknown | Shot down by 803 Sqn Skua |
| 8-10-39 | Dornier Do-18 | Off Aberdeen | Küstenstaffel 2./KüFlGr 506 | Ltn Hornkuhl | Shot down by unknown fighter |
| 9-10-39 | Junkers Ju-88 | North Sea | Kampfstaffel 1./I./KG 30 | Oblt Kahl | Shot down by fighter |
| 16-10-39 | Junkers Ju-88 | Firth of Forth | Kampfstaffel 1./I./KG 30 | Ltn H. von Riesen | Shot down by 603 Sqn Spitfire |
| 16-10-39 | Junkers Ju-88 | Firth of Forth | Gruppenstab I./KG 30 | Hptm H. Pohle | Shot down by 602 Sqn Spitfire |
| 17-10-39 | Junkers Ju-88 | Hoy, Orkney | Kampfstaffel 1./I./KG 30 4D+EK | Oblt Flaemig | Shot down by AA fire |
| 21-10-39 | Heinkel He-115 | Off Aberdeen | Küstenstaffel 1./KüFlGr 406 | Oblt Peinemann | Shot down by unknown fighter |
| 28-10-39 | Heinkel He-111 | Humbie, Ebgh | Kampfgeschwader KG 26 1H+JA | Uffz K. Lehmkuhl | Shot down by 602 & 603 Sqn Spitfires |
| 6-12-39 | Heinkel He-111 | Moray Firth | Aufklärungsgruppe 1(F)./122 | Fw H. Petersen | Unknown, probably AA fire |
| 7-12-39 | Heinkel He-111 | Tay estuary | Kampfgeschwader KG 26 | Ltn A. Luneburg | Shot down by 603 & 72 Squadrons |
| 7-12-39 | Heinkel He-111 | Tay estuary | Kampfgeschwader KG 26 | Uffz H. Zenger | Shot down by 603 & 72 Squadrons |
| 22-12-39 | Heinkel He-111 | Isle of May | Kampfgeschwader KG 26 | Unknown | Shot down by 602 Sqn Spitfires |
| 1-1-40 | Junkers Ju-88 | Fetlar, Shetland | Kampfstaffel 1./I./KG 30 | Ogefr Kasiske | Shot down by 152 Sqn Gladiator SFF |
| 13-1-40 | Heinkel He-111 | Fife Ness, Ebgh | Aufklärungsstaffel 1(F)./AufklGr 122 | Unknown | Shot down by 602 & 111 Squadrons |
| 17-1-40 | Heinkel He-111 | Fair Isle | Wettererkundungsstaffel 1./ObdL | Ltn Karl H.Thurz | Shot down by 43 Sqn Hurricanes |
| 19-1-40 | Heinkel He-111 | Off Aberdeen | Aufklärungsgruppe 1(F)./ObdL | LtdR Johann Fokuhl | Shot down by 603 Sqn Spitfires |
| 3-2-40 | Junkers Ju-88 | Moray Firth | Kampfstaffel I./KG 30 | Hptm H. Rosenthal POW | AA Fire from minesweeper |

| Date | Aircraft | Location | Unit | Crew | Cause |
|---|---|---|---|---|---|
| 9-2-40 | Heinkel He-111 | North Berwick | Kampfgeschwader KG 26 | Uffz H. Mayer | Shot down by 602 Sqn Spitfire |
| 22-2-40 | Heinkel He-111 | Coldingham | Kampfgeschwader KG 26 | Unknown | Shot down by 602 & 72 Sqn Spitfires |
| 27-2-40 | Heinkel He-111 | Off Dunbar | Kampfgeschwader KG 26 | Oblt Heirich | Shot down by 609 Sqn Spitfire |
| 7-3-40 | Heinkel He-111 | Off Aberdeen | Aufklärungsstaffel 1(F)./AufklGr ObdL | Unknown | Shot down by 603 Sqn Spitfire |
| 8-3-40 | Junkers Ju-88 | Off Orkney | Kampfstaffel 2./I./KG 30 | Oblt F. von Sicharhoff | Shot down by 111 Sqn Hurricane |
| 20-2-40 | Heinkel He-111 | Off Orkney | Kampfstaffel 6./II/KG26 | Hptm O. Andreas | Shot down by 43 Sqn Hurricane |
| 3-4-40 | Junkers Ju-88 | Off east coast | Kampfstaffel 5./II./KG 30 | Oblt Karl Overweg | Shot down by 204 Sqn Sunderland |
| 8-4-40 | Heinkel He-111 | Scapa Flow | Kampfstaffel 4./KG 26 | Oblt Alfred Donke | Shot down by 43 Sqn Hurricane |
| 8-4-40 | Heinkel He-111 | Scapa Flow | Kampfstaffel 6./KG 26 | Uffz M. Hofer | Shot down by 43 Sqn Hurricane |
| 8-4-40 | Heinkel He-111 | Wick Airfield | Kampfstaffel 6./KG 26 | Ltn Kurt Weigel | Shot down by 43 Sqn Hurricane |
| 9-4-40 | Junkers Ju-88 | Scapa Flow | Kampfstaffel III./KG 30 | Unknown | Shot down by AA fire |
| 9-4-40 | Junkers Ju-88 | Scapa Flow | Kampfstaffel III./KG 30 | Unknown | Shot down by AA fire |
| 9-4-40 | Junkers Ju-88 | Scapa Flow | Kampfstaffel IV./KG 30 | Unknown | Shot down by AA fire |
| 9-4-40 | Junkers Ju-88 | Scapa Flow | Kampfstaffel III./KG 30 | Unknown | Shot down by AA fire |
| 9-4-40 | Heinkel He-111 | Scapa Flow | Kampfgeschwader KG 26 3./ObdL | Unknown | Shot down by AA fire |
| 10-4-40 | Heinkel He-111 | Scapa Flow | Kampfgeschwader KG 100 | Unknown | Shot down by AA fire |
| 10-4-40 | Heinkel He-111 | Scapa Flow | Aufklärungsstaffel 3(F)./AufklGr ObdL | Oblt K. Heinz | Shot down by 43 Sqn Hurricane |
| 10-4-40 | Dornier Do-18 | Off Orkney | [Küstenstaffel?] 2./Küstenfliegergruppe 106 | Unknown | Shot down by AA fire |

| Date | Type | Location | Unit / Code | Crew / Captain | Details |
|---|---|---|---|---|---|
| 10-4-40 | Heinkel He-111 | Scapa Flow | Kampfstaffel 2./I./KG 26 | Oblt H. Müller | Shot down by AA fire |
| 10-4-40 | Heinkel He-111 | Scapa Flow | Kampfstaffel 4./II./KG 26 | Oblt H. Vogel | Shot down by 605 Sqn Hurricane |
| 10-4-40 | Heinkel He-111 | Scapa Flow | Kampfstaffel I./I./KG 26 | Fw F. Bausacher | Shot down by 111 Sqn Hurricane |
| 10-4-40 | Heinkel He-111 | Scapa Flow | Kampfstaffel 1./I./KG 26 | Oblt O. Housselle | Shot down by 605 Sqn Hurricane |
| 10-4-40 | Junkers Ju-88 | Scapa Flow | Kampfstaffel 2./I./KG 30 | Obfw W. Brünn | Shot down by AA fire |
| 10-4-40 | Junkers Ju-88 | Scapa Flow | Kampfstaffel 4./II./KG 30 | Ltn H. Hohendahl | Shot down by AA fire |
| 11-4-40 | Dornier Do-18 | Off Fraserburgh | Küstenfliegergruppe 106 | Unknown | Shot down by 602 Sqn Spitfires |
| 11-4-40 | Dornier Do-18 | Off Fraserburgh | Küstenfliegergruppe 106 | Ltn Helmut Kuhl | Shot down by 602 Sqn Spitfires |
| 11-4-40 | Dornier Do-18 | Off Fraserburgh | Küstenfliegergruppe 106 | Unknown | Shot down by 602 Sqn Spitfires |
| 25-4-40 | Dornier Do-18 | Off Shetland | Küstenstaffel 2./KüFlGr 406 | Unknown | Shot down by 43 Sqn Hurricane |
| 4-6-40 | Dornier Do-18 | Off Sumburgh | Küstenstaffel 2./KFlüGr 906 | Ltn H. Weinlig | Shot down by 43 Sqn Hurricane |
| 26-6-40 | Heinkel He-111 | Near Turnhouse | Kampfstaffel 3./I./KG 26 | Hptm H. Schwilden | Shot down by 602 Sqn Spitfires |
| 26-6-40 | Heinkel He-111 | Firth of Forth | Kampfstaffel 3./I./KG 26 | Uffz H. Wilm | Shot down by 602 & 603 Sqn Spitfires |
| 26-6-40 | Heinkel He-111 | Off Aberdeen | Kampfstaffel 9./III./KG 26 | Ltn H. Hauck | Shot down by 603 Sqn Spitfires |
| 3-7-40 | Junkers Ju-88 | Off Montrose | Kampfstaffel 8./III./KG 30 | Fw Heidinger | Shot down by 603 Sqn Spitfires |

| Date | Aircraft | Location | Unit | Crew | Cause |
|---|---|---|---|---|---|
| 3-7-40 | Junkers Ju-88 | Off Stonehaven | Kampfstaffel 8./III./KG 30 | Hptm Schulze-Langsdorf | Shot down by 603 Sqn Spitfires |
| 3-7-40 | Junkers Ju-88 | Off Peterhead | Kampfstaffel 8./III./KG 30 | Unknown | Shot down by 603 Sqn Spitfires |
| 3-7-40 | Junkers Ju-88 | Firth of Forth | Kampfstaffel 8./III./KG 30 | Ltn Meinhold | Shot down by 603 Sqn Spitfires |
| 6-7-40 | Messerschmitt Bf-110 | Off Aberdeen | Aufklärungsstaffel ./(F)/AufklGr ObdL | Ltn Brix | Shot down by 603 Sqn Spitfires |
| 7-7-40 | Junkers Ju-88 | Firth of Forth | Kampfstaffel 1./I./KG 30 | Unknown | Shot down by AA fire |
| 8-7-40 | Heinkel He-111 | Firth of Forth | Aufklärungsstaffel 1(F)./AufklGr 120 | Unknown | Shot down by 602 Sqn Spitfires |
| 12-7-40 | Heinkel He-111 | Aberdeen | Kampfstaffel 9./III./KG 26 | Ltn H. Huck | Shot down by 603 Sqn Spitfires |
| 15-7-40 | Heinkel He-111 | Off Peterhead | Kampfstaffel 3./I./KG 26 1H+RK | Oblt O. Hollmann | Shot down by 603 Sqn Spitfires |
| 16-7-40 | Heinkel He-111 | Off Fraserburgh | Kampfgeschwader KG 26 | Unknown | Shot down by 603 Sqn Spitfires |
| 17-7-40 | Heinkel He-111 | Off Fraserburgh | Kampfstaffel III./KG 26 1H+KT | Oblt G. Lorenz | Shot down by 603 Sqn Spitfires |
| 20-7-40 | Dornier Do-17 | Off Peterhead | Aufklärungsstaffel 1(F)./AufklGr 120 | Unknown | Shot down by 603 Sqn Spitfires |
| 25-7-40 | Heinkel He-111 | Off Fraserburgh | Kampfgeschwader KG 26 | Unknown | Shot down by 603 Sqn Spitfires |
| 30-7-40 | Heinkel He-111 | Off Montrose | Kampfstaffel III./KG 26 | Uffz H. Grieshaber | Shot down by 603 Sqn Spitfires |
| 1-8-40 | Junkers Ju-88 | Near Edinburgh | Kampfstaffel 1./I./KG 30 | Unknown | Shot down by AA fire |
| 2-8-40 | Heinkel He-115 | Off Stonehaven | Küstenfliegergruppe 3./506 | LtzSee H. Richter | Shot down by AA fire |

| Date | Type | Location | Unit / Code | Crew / Captain | Details |
|---|---|---|---|---|---|
| 2-8-40 | Heinkel He-115 | Off Stonehaven | Küstenfliegergruppe 3./506 | LtzSee W. Starke | Shot down by AA fire |
| 2-8-40 | Heinkel He-115 | Off Stonehaven | Küstenfliegergruppe 3./506 | Uffz Heinz Löffler | Shot down by 235 Sqn Blenheim |
| 2-8-40 | Heinkel He-115 | Off Stonehaven | Küstenfliegergruppe 3./506 | Fw Siegfreid Gast | Shot down by SS *Highlander's* Projector |
| 15-8-40 | Heinkel He-115 | Arbroath | Küstenfliegergruppe 506 | Obfw R Holfert | Crashed |
| 23-8-40 | Heinkel He-111 | Sumburgh | Kampfgeschwader KG 26 | Unknown | Shot down by 232 Sqn Hurricanes |
| 11-9-40 | Heinkel He-111 | Moray Firth | Führungskette, X.Fliegerkorps P4+BA | Hptm R. Kowalewski | Crashed after engine failure |
| 16-9-40 | Heinkel He-115 | Off Aberdour | Küstenfliegergruppe I./906 8L+GH | LtzSee H. Aldus | Force-landed |
| 16-9-40 | Heinkel He-115 | Off Eyemouth | Küstenstaffel 3./KüFlGr 506 | Unknown | Shot down by AA fire |
| 2-10-40 | Heinkel He-115 | Off Peterhead | Küstenstaffel 1./KüFlGr 506 | LtzSee G. Lenz | Shot down by 254 Sqn Blenheims |
| 8-10-40 | Dornier Do-17 | Rattray Head | Aufklärungsstaffel 2(F)./AufklGr 22 | Ltn E. von Eichstedt | Crashed after engine failure |
| 11-10-40 | Junkers Ju-88 | Lossiemouth | Kampfgeschwader KG 30 | Unknown | Shot down by 20 OTU air gunner |
| 26-10-40 | Heinkel He-115 | Off Fraserburgh | Küstenstaffel 1./KüFlGr 506 | Ltn K. Kemper | Shot down by 603 Sqn Spitfires |
| 13-11-40 | Heinkel He-111 | Off Aberdeen | Aufklärungsstaffel 1(F)./AufklGr 120 | Oblt A.Fuhrmann | Shot down by 111 Sqn Hurricanes |
| 26-12-40 | Junkers Ju-88 | Scapa Flow | Aufklärungsstaffel 3(F)./AufklGr 22 | Ltn K. Schipp | Shot down by 804 Sqn Martlet |
| 17-1-41 | Heinkel He-111 | Fair Isle | Wettererkundungsstaffel 1./ObdL | Ltn K.Thurz | Shot down by 3 Sqn Hurricane |

| Date | Aircraft | Location | Unit | Crew | Remarks |
|---|---|---|---|---|---|
| 20-1-41 | Heinkel He-111 | North Sea | Wettererkundungsstaffel 5 | Fw G. Hummel | Shot down by 43 Sqn Hurricane |
| 12-2-41 | Junkers Ju-88 | Off east coast | Aufklärungsstaffel 1(F)./AufklGr 120 | Unknown | Shot down by AA fire |
| 13-2-41 | Junkers Ju-88 | Monifieth | Aufklärungsstaffel 1(F)./AufklGr 120 | Fw W. Presia | Crashed due to weather |
| 20-2-41 | Heinkel He-111 | Moray Firth | Kampfgeschwader I./KG 26 | Ltn E. Hofmann | AA fire from ship "Stella Rigler" |
| 23-2-41 | Heinkel He-115 | Moray Firth | Küstenstaffel 3./KüFlGr 506 | LtzSee H. Buchmann | Shot down by AA fire |
| 1-3-41 | Heinkel He-115 | Off Whitehills | Kampfstaffel 2./I./KG26 1H+BK | Oblt Hatto Kühn | Shot down by AA fire |
| 4-3-41 | Junkers Ju-88 | Off Westray | Aufklärungsstaffel 1(F)./AufklGr 120 | Fw J. Mischke | Shot down by 253 Sqn Hurricanes |
| 7-3-41 | Heinkel He-111 | Off Buddon | Kampfgeschwader I/KG 26 | Uffz K. Seeland | Struck mast of ship and crashed |
| 11-3-41 | Heinkel He-111 | Off west coast | Kampfgeschwader KG 26 | Unknown | Shot down by AA fire |
| 13-3-41 | Heinkel He-111 | Clydebank | Unknown | Unknown | Shot down by AA fire |
| 23-3-41 | Messerschmitt Bf-110 | Sullom Voe | Aufklärungsstaffel ./(F)/AufklGr ObdL | Uffz K.Rudigar | Shot down by AA fire |
| 31-3-41 | Junkers Ju-88 | Off Peterhead | Aufklärungsstaffel 1(F)./AufklGr 124 | Oblt G. Rosenfeld | Shot down by 43 Sqn Hurricane |
| 8-4-41 | Heinkel He-111 | Fife Ness | Kampfgeschwader I/KG 26 | Uffz H. Braucks | Crashed due to engine failure |
| 16-4-41 | Focke-Wulf Fw-200 | Off Aberdeen | Kampfstaffel 1./I./KG 40 F8+AH | Oblt H. Daerner | Shot down by 252 Sqn Beaufighter |
| 17-4-41 | Focke-Wulf Fw-200 | Off Shetland | Kampfstaffel 1./I./KG 40 F8 + FH | Oblt P. Kalus | Shot down by AA fire |
| 24-4-41 | Junkers Ju-88 | Firth of Forth | Aufklärungsstaffel 1(F)./AufklGr 124 | Oblt H. Petran | Shot down by AA fire |

| Date | Type | Location | Unit / Code | Crew / Captain | Details |
|------|------|----------|-------------|----------------|---------|
| 29-4-41 | Focke-Wulf Fw-200 | Off Shetland | Kampfstaffel 1./I./KG 40 F8 + HH | Oblt R. Schelcher | Shot down by AA fire |
| 5-5-41 | Junkers Ju-88 | Greenock area | Küstenstaffel 2./KüFlGr 106 | Hptm G. Hansmann | Shot down by 141 Sqn Defiant |
| 5-5-41 | Junkers Ju-88 | Borders area | Kampfgeschwader KG 30 | Unknown | Shot down by 141 Sqn Defiant |
| 6-5-41 | Heinkel He-111 | Borders area | Unknown | Unknown | Shot down by 141 Sqn Defiant |
| 7-5-41 | Junkers Ju-88 | Tay estuary | Aufklärungsstaffel 1(F)./AufklGr 124 | Ltn A. König | Shot down by 43 Sqn Hurricane |
| 10-5-41 | Messerschmitt Bf-110 | Renfrewshire | Unknown code VJ+OQ | R. Hess | Crashed after pilot bailed out |
| 17-5-41 | Junkers Ju-88 | Off Aberdeen | Aufklärungsstaffel 1(F)./AufklGr 124 | Obfw E. Schneider | Crashed due to engine failure |
| 28-5-41 | Junkers Ju-88 | Riccarton | 2/Aufklärungsgruppe | Ltn F. Gortan | Shot down by 43 Sqn Hurricane |
| 28-5-41 | Junkers Ju-88 | Isle of Iona | StabII/ Kampfgeschwader KG54 | Uffz H. Mandl | Shot down by 43 Sqn Hurricane |
| 5-6-41 | Heinkel He-111 | Aberdeen | Kampfgeschwader I./KG 26 | Obfw E. Burghof | Shot down by AA fire |
| 7-6-41 | Junkers Ju-88 | Loch Ewe | Kampfgeschwader II./KG 30 | Oblt A. Wolf | Shot down by AA fire |
| 8-6-41 | Junkers Ju-88 | Off Eyemouth | Kampfgeschwader II./KG 30 | Ltn A. Hick | Shot down by 43 Sqn Hurricane |
| 12-6-41 | Junkers Ju-88 | Loch Ewe | Kampfgeschwader I./KG 30 | Gefr Ernst Füllner | Shot down by 500 Sqn Blenheim |
| 13-6-41 | Heinkel He-111 | Off Peterhead | Kampfgeschwader I./KG 26 | Oblt W. Rohländer | Shot down by AA fire |
| 25-6-41 | Heinkel He-111 | Off east coast | Kampfstaffel 1./I./KG 26  1H + BH | Fw F. Lehmann | Shot down by AA fire |
| 25-6-41 | Heinkel He-111 | Off east coast | Kampfstaffel 1./I./KG 26  1H + AK | Uffz W. Kerney | Shot down by AA fire |

| Date | Aircraft | Location | Unit | Crew | Cause |
|---|---|---|---|---|---|
| 25-6-41 | Heinkel He-111 | Off east coast | Kampfstaffel 1./I./KG 26 1H + MK | Oblt H. Osswald | Shot down by AA fire |
| 26-6-41 | Junkers Ju-88 | Off Fraserburgh | Kampfgeschwader IV./KG 30 | Gefr H. Schröder | Crashed after engine failure |
| 9-7-41 | Heinkel He-111 | Off Aberdeen | Kampfgeschwader I./KG 26 | Unknown | Shot down by AA fire |
| 11-7-41 | Junkers Ju-88 | Off east coast | Aufklärungsstaffel 1(F)./AufklGr 120 | Uffz L. Husskönig | Shot down by AA fire |
| 14-7-41 | Junkers Ju-88 | Near Montrose | Küstenstaffel 1./KüGr 506 | LtzSee E. Becker | Shot down by AA fire |
| 17-7-41 | Junkers Ju-88 | Off Fraserburgh | [Küstenstaffel?] 1./Küstenfliegergruppe 506 | Unknown | Shot down by AA fire |
| 17-7-41 | Junkers Ju-88 | Off Fraserburgh | [Küstenstaffel?] 3./Küstenfliegergruppe 606 | Unknown | Shot down by AA fire |
| 18-7-41 | Junkers Ju-88 | Off east coast | Küstenstaffel 1./KüFlGr 506 | Unknown | Shot down by 43 Sqn Hurricane |
| 19-7-41 | Heinkel He-111 | Off east coast | Kampfgeschwader I./KG 26 1H+HL | Ogefr W. Melzer | Shot down by AA fire |
| 24-7-41 | Junkers Ju-88 | Firth of Forth | Aufklärungsstaffel 1(F)./AufklGr 120 | Uffz W. Romer | Shot down by 43 Sqn Hurricane |
| 2-8-41 | Junkers Ju-88 | Off Aberdeen | Küstenstaffel 1./KüFlGr 506 | Unknown | Shot down by AA fire |
| 14-8-41 | Heinkel He-111 | Off east coast | Kampfgeschwader I./KG 26 | Fw F. Bollinger | Shot down by 43 Sqn Hurricane |
| 5-9-41 | Junkers Ju-88 | Stonehaven | 2/Küstenfliegergruppe 906 | Uffz W. Dreyhage | Flew into a hill. |
| 6-9-41 | Junkers Ju-88 | Off east coast | Kampfgeschwader I./KG 30 | Unknown | Shot down by 43 Sqn Hurricane |
| 13-9-41 | Heinkel He-111 | Firth of Forth | Kampfgeschwader I./KG 26 1H+AL | Ltn R. Machbert | Shot down by AA fire |

| Date | Type | Location | Unit / Code | Crew / Captain | Details |
|---|---|---|---|---|---|
| 13-9-41 | Heinkel He-111 | Firth of Forth | Kampfgeschwader I./KG 26  1H+KL | Stfw E. Bergemann | Shot down by AA fire |
| 29-9-41 | Junkers Ju-88 | Off east coast | Kampfgeschwader I./KG 30 | Gefr H. Wendt | Shot down by AA fire |
| 23-11-41 | Heinkel He-111 | Firth of Forth | Stab/Kampfgeschwader KG26 | Oblt B. Pape | Shot down by AA fire |
| 18-12-41 | Junkers Ju-88 | Off Shetland | Wettererkundungsstaffel 1 | Unknown | Crashed after engine failure |
| 22-12-41 | Junkers Ju-88 | Off east coast | Aufklärungsstaffel 1(F)./AufklGr 120 | Oblt A. Kober | Shot down by AA fire |
| 29-12-41 | Junkers Ju-88 | Off east coast | Küstenstaffel 1./KüFlGr 506 | Unknown | Shot down by AA fire |
| 11-3-42 | Heinkel He-111 | Moray Firth | Kampfgeschwader I./KG 26  1H+CA | Ltn J. Greil | Shot down by AA fire |
| 31-3-42 | Junkers Ju-88 | Off Aberdeen | Aufklärungsstaffel 1(F)./AufklGr 124 | Uffz A. Brünninghof | Shot down by 43 Sqn Hurricane |
| 1-4-42 | Heinkel He-111 | Moray Firth | Kampfgeschwader I./KG 26  1H+GL | Ltn K. Postl | Shot down by AA fire |
| 13-4-42 | Junkers Ju-88 | Off east coast | Erprobungsstaffel.St./ Kampfgeschwader KG 30 | Uffz B. Beissert | Shot down by AA fire |
| 25-4-42 | Heinkel He-115 | Off Aberdeen | Lufttorpedostaffel 1./KüFlGr 906 | Hptm E. Peukert | Shot down by 43 Sqn Hurricane |
| 26-4-42 | Junkers Ju-88 | Moray Firth | Küstenstaffel 1./KüFlGr 506 | Unknown | Shot down by AA fire |
| 27-4-42 | Heinkel He-111 | Off Peterhead | Wettererkundungsstaffel 1 | Unknown | Shot down by 416 Sqn Spitfire |
| 27-5-42 | Heinkel He-111 | Moray Firth | Wettererkundungsstaffel 1 | Unknown | Shot down by 125 Sqn Beaufighter |
| 8-6-42 | Bv-138 C-1 | Off Shetland | Küstenstaffel 2./KüFlGr 406 | Ltn E. Stieper | Shot down by 248 Sqn Beaufighter |
| 11-6-42 | Junkers Ju-88 | Off east coast | Aufklärungsstaffel 1(F)./AufklGr 122 | Unknown | Shot down by AA fire |
| 11-6-42 | Junkers Ju-88 | Off Peterhead | Wettererkundungsstaffel 2 | Unknown | Shot down by 416 Sqn Spitfire |

| Date | Aircraft | Location | Unit | Crew | Fate |
|---|---|---|---|---|---|
| 22-8-42 | Bv-138 C-1 | Off Shetland | Küstenstaffel 1./KüFlGr 706 | Oblt S. Schwartz | Shot down by 248 Sqn Beaufighter |
| 16-9-42 | Heinkel He-111 | Off Fair Isle | Führungskette KG 26 | Obfw I. Jakob | Shot down by 248 Sqn Beaufighter |
| 4-11-42 | Junkers Ju-88 | Off Aberdeen | Wettererkundungsstaffel 1./ObdL | Ltn R. Elson | Shot down by AA fire |
| 10-11-42 | Junkers Ju-88 | Moray Firth | Wettererkundungsstaffel 1./ObdL | Hptm K. Jonas | Shot down by AA fire |
| 25-12-42 | Junkers Ju-88 | Off Shetland | Aufklärungsstaffel 1(F)./ObdL | Unknown | Shot down by 248 Sqn Beaufighter |
| 24-3-43 | Junkers Ju-88 | Sumburgh Head | Aufklärungsstaffel 1(F)./ AufklGr 120 | Obstlt S. Otternberg | Shot down by 234 Sqn Spitfire |
| 25-3-43 | Junkers Ju-88 | Firth of Forth | Kampfgeschwader I./KG 30 | Fw Hans Reis | Shot down by AA fire |
| 25-3-43 | Dornier Do-217 E-4 | Dumfriesshire | Kampfgeschwader 7./KG2 | Oblt M. Pischke | Crashed after engine fire |
| 25-3-43 | Junkers Ju-88 | Near Edinburgh | Kampfgeschwader I./KG 30 | Oblt F. Forster | Flew into Hare Hill, Balerno |
| 25-3-43 | Junkers Ju-88 | Berwickshire | Kampfgeschwader V./KG 30 | Obstlt Rogge | Crashed near Earlston, Berwickshire |
| 25-3-43 | Junkers Ju-88 | Edinburgh | Kampfgeschwader 4/KG 6 | Oblt J. Weissgerber | Shot down by AA fire |
| 8-7-43 | BV-138 C-1 | Off Shetland | Küstenstaffel 2./KüFlGr 406 K6+IK | Oblt R. Schumacher | Shot down by 404 Sqn Beaufighter |
| 8-7-43 | Junkers Ju-88 | Off Shetland | Aufklärungsstaffel 1(F)./ AufklGr 120 | Oblt H. Geist | Shot down by FAA 801 Sqn Martlet |
| 28-7-43 | BV-138 C-1 | Off Shetland | Aufklärungsstaffel 1(F)./SAufklGr 131 | Fw K. Kopatzki | Shot down by 404 Sqn Beaufighters |
| 28-7-43 | Bv-138 C-1 | Off Shetland | Aufklärungsstaffel 1(F)./SAufklGr 131 | Fw F. Siegmann | Shot down by 404 Sqn Beaufighters |
| 28-7-43 | Bv-138 C-1 | Off Shetland | Aufklärungsstaffel 1(F)./SAufklGr 131 | Uffz H. Krieger | Shot down by 404 Sqn Beaufighters |
| 28-7-43 | Bv-138 C-1 | Off Shetland | Aufklärungsstaffel 1(F)./SAufklGr 131 | Uffz G. Feddersen | Shot down by 404 Sqn Beaufighters |

| Date | Type | Location | Unit / Code | Crew / Captain | Details |
|---|---|---|---|---|---|
| 28-7-43 | Bv-138 C-1 | Off Shetland | Aufklärungsstaffel 1(F)./SAufklGr 130 | Stabsfw H. Olschewsky | Shot down by FAA 801 Sqn Martlet |
| 27-8-43 | Junkers Ju-88 | Firth of Tay | Aufklärungsstaffel 1(F)./ AufklGr 120 | Ltn A. Meder | Shot down by AA fire |
| 6-9-43 | Junkers Ju-88 | Lerwick | Aufklärungsstaffel 1(F)./ AufklGr 120 | Oblt H. Nemitz | Shot down by AA fire over Lerwick |
| 17-11-43 | Messerschmitt Bf-109 | Scapa Flow | Aufklärungsstaffel 1(F)./ AufklGr 120 | Hptm W. Lerch | Shot down by AA fire |
| 22-11-43 | Heinkel He-177 | Off Shetland | Kampfgeschwader KG 40 | Unknown | Shot down by 307 (Polish) Sqn Mosquito |
| 26-11-43 | Junkers Ju-88 | Off Shetland | Aufklärungsstaffel 1(F)./ AufklGr 22 | Obfw Max Prüfert | Shot down by 307 (Polish) Sqn Mosquito |
| 2-12-43 | Junkers Ju-88 | Sumburgh Head | Aufklärungsstaffel 1(F)./ AufklGr 22 | Hptm F. Bock | Shot down by 453 Sqn Spitfire |
| 8-12-43 | Junkers Ju-88 | Off Shetland | Aufklärungsstaffel 1(F)./ AufklGr 33 | Unknown | Shot down by 307 (Polish) Sqn Mosquito |
| 10-12-43 | Junkers Ju-88 | Off Shetland | Aufklärungsstaffel 1(F)./ AufklGr 120 | Oblt K. Bender | Shot down by 333 (RNAF) Sqn Mosquito |
| 22-2-44 | Messerschmitt Bf-109 | Off Orkney | Aufklärungsstaffel 1(F)./ AufklGr 120 | Oblt H. Quednau | Shot down by 602 Sqn Spitfire |
| 5-3-44 | Junkers Ju-88 | Off Lerwick | Aufklärungsstaffel 1(F)./ AufklGr 120 | Oblt A. Cardaun | Shot down by AA fire |
| 22-4-44 | Junkers Ju-188 F-1 | Off Orkney | Aufklärungsstaffel 1(F)./ AufklGr 120 | Uffz G. Poltrock | Shot down by 504 Sqn Spitfires |
| 20-6-44 | Junkers Ju-188 F-1 | Rothes, Moray | Aufklärungsstaffel 1(F)./ AufklGr 120 | Oblt Winne | Flew into Hill north-west of Rothes |

| Date | Aircraft | Location | Unit | Crew | Notes |
|---|---|---|---|---|---|
| 25-10-44 | Junkers Ju-52 See | Off Aberdeen | Seetransportstaffel 2 | Unknown | Ditched in sea, crew defecting |
| 26-12-44 | Messerschmitt Bf-109 | Dyce, Aberdeen | 7/Jagdgeschwader 77 | Uffz W. Drude | Crash-landed, pilot defecting |
| 29-12-44 | Junkers Ju-188 F-1 | Loch Broom | Aufklärungsstaffel 1(F)./ AufklGr 120 | Oblt Neugebauer | Crashed after engine failure |
| 29-12-44 | Junkers Ju-188 F-1 | Scapa Flow | Aufklärungsstaffel 1(F)./ AufklGr 120 | Unknown | Shot down by 611 Sqn Spitfires |
| 4-1-45 | Junkers Ju-188 F-1 | Off east coast | Aufklärungsstaffel 1(F)./ AufklGr 120 | Unknown | Shot down by AA fire |
| 21-4-45 | Junkers Ju-88 A-17 | Off east coast | Lufttorpedostaffel II./KG 26 | Oblt K. Küchenmeister | Shot down by Banff SW Mosquito |
| 21-4-45 | Junkers Ju-88 A-17 | Off east coast | Lufttorpedostaffel II./KG 26 | Ltn G. Schäfer | Shot down by Banff SW Mosquito |
| 21-4-45 | Junkers Ju-88 A-17 | Off east coast | Lufttorpedostaffel II./KG 26 | Uffz K. Langendorf | Shot down by Banff SW Mosquito |
| 21-4-45 | Junkers Ju-88 A-17 | Off east coast | Lufttorpedostaffel II./KG 26 | Uffz K. Walldorf | Shot down by Banff SW Mosquito |
| 21-4-45 | Junkers Ju-88 A-17 | Off east coast | Lufttorpedostaffel II./KG 26 | Oblt F. Dombrowkski | Shot down by Banff SW Mosquito |
| 21-4-45 | Junkers Ju-88 A-17 | Off east coast | Lufttorpedostaffel II./KG 26 | Obfw Zimmermann | Shot down by Banff SW Mosquito |
| 21-4-45 | Junkers Ju-188 F-1 | Off east coast | Lufttorpedostaffel III./KG 26 | Oblt F. Ebert | Shot down by Banff SW Mosquito |
| 21-4-45 | Junkers Ju-188 F-1 | Off east coast | Lufttorpedostaffel III./KG 26 | Obfw H. Kunze | Shot down by Banff SW Mosquito |
| 21-4-45 | Junkers Ju-188 F-1 | Off east coast | Lufttorpedostaffel III./KG 26 | Uffz Behrend | Shot down by Banff SW Mosquito |

| Date | Type | Location | Unit / Code | Crew / Captain | Details |
|---|---|---|---|---|---|
| 21-4-45 | Junkers Ju-188 F-1 | Off east coast | Lufttorpedostaffel III./KG 26 | Uffz Weyhrauch | Shot down by Banff SW Mosquito |
| 21-4-45 | Junkers Ju-188 F-1 | Off east coast | Lufttorpedostaffel III./KG 26 | Crew posted missing | Shot down by Banff SW Mosquito |
| 21-4-45 | Junkers Ju-188 F-1 | Off east coast | Lufttorpedostaffel III./KG 26 | Crew posted missing | Shot down by Banff SW Mosquito |
| 21-4-45 | Junkers Ju-188 F-1 | Off east coast | Lufttorpedostaffel III./KG 26 | Crew posted missing | Shot down by Banff SW Mosquito |
| 21-4-45 | Junkers Ju-188 F-1 | Off east coast | Lufttorpedostaffel III./KG 26 | Crew posted missing | Shot down by 333 (RNAF) Sqn Mosquito |

# Bibliography

**BOOKS**

Bowyer, Chaz. *Mosquito at War*, London, Ian Allan, 1973

    *Beaufighter at War*, London, Ian Allan, 1976

    *History of the RAF*, Middlesex, The Hamlyn Publishing Group Ltd, 1977

    *Coastal Command at War*, London, Ian Allan, 1979

Brown, Eric. *Wings of the Luftwaffe*, London, Pilot Press Ltd, 1977

Buckton, Henry. *Birth of the Few*, Shrewsbury, Airlife Publishing Ltd, 1998

Coughlin, Tom. *The Dangerous Sky*, Toronto, The Ryerson Press, 1968

Deighton, Len. *Fighter*, London, Jonathan Cape Ltd, 1977

Dey, George Allan *Fraserburgh at War*, Aberdeen, BCP-AUP, 1990

Earl, David W. *Hell on High Ground*, Shrewsbury, Airlife Publishing Ltd, 1999

Foxley-Norris, C. *A Lighter Shade of Blue*, Shepperton, Surrey, Ian Allan Ltd, 1978

Harris, Paul. *Aberdeen at War*, Manchester, Archive Publications, 1987

Hastings, Max. *Bomber Command*, London, Michael Joseph Ltd, 1979

    *Armageddon*, London, Macmillan, 2004

Hooton, E.R. *Phoenix Triumphant*, London, Arms and Armour Press, 1994

Hughes, Jim. *A Steep Turn to the Stars*, Elgin, Benevenagh Books, 1981

Nimmo, Ian. *Scotland at War*, Cheshire, Archive Publications Ltd, 1989

Overy, Richard. *Why the Allies Won*, London, Pimlico, 1995

Paul, Wolfgang. *Hermann Göring*, London, Arms and Armour Press, 1998

Price, Alfred. *Blitz on Britain*, London, Ian Allan, 1977
    *Luftwaffe Data Book*, London, Greenhill Books, 1997
    *Last Year of the Luftwaffe*, London, Wren's Park Publishing, 1999
Ramsey, W.G. *Blitz Then and Now*, Vol 3, London, Battle of Britain Prints
    International Ltd, 1990
Robertson, Seona, and Wilson, Les. *Scotland's War*, Edinburgh, Mainstream
    Publishing, 1995
Smith, David J. *Action Stations Number 7*, Cambridge, Patrick Stephens Ltd, 1983
Sweetman, John. *Tirpitz: Hunting the Beast*, Gloucestershire, Sutton Publishing,
    2000

## DOCUMENTS AND ARTICLES

'Scotland Under Fire. Note on Enemy Air Attacks from October 1939 to February
    29 1944.'
The Press Office, St Andrew's House, Edinburgh, 13 October, 1944
Available from The Second World War Experience Centre, 5 Feast Field, Horsforth,
    Leeds LS18 4TJ


'Return on Analysis of Casualties of raids on Clydeside on 13/14 and 14/15 March
    1941.'
Glasgow City Corporation, Glasgow, 1947
Available from Glasgow City Archives & Special Collections, Records of the Town
    Clerk


'Raids on Clydeside, Office of the Regional Commissioner, Scotland.'
Report of the Office of Public Works, 1938–1948, Published by Glasgow City
    Corporation
Available from Glasgow City Archives & Special Collections, Records of the Town
    Clerk, The Mitchell Library, 210 North Street, Glasgow G3 7DN


'City of Aberdeen Air Raid Warnings and Enemy Action, 26 June to 30 April 1945.'
    Aberdeen City Council, September 1946.
Available from Aberdeen City Libraries, Central Library, Aberdeen City Council,
    Rosemount Viaduct, Aberdeen AB25 1GW


'List of civilian casualties in Aberdeen Air Raids, 12 July 1940 to 21 April 1945.'
    Aberdeen City Council, September 1946.
Available from Aberdeen City Libraries

'A Bombing Disaster.' Jim Davidson, *Leopard* magazine, Inverurie, 1995

'The First of the Many.' Andy Saunders, *After the Battle* magazine, issue 42, May 1983. Battle of Britain Prints International Ltd, London, 1983

## ONLINE SOURCES

Aviation History Society, Norway: www.ahs.no

Axis History Forum: forum.axishistory.com

Battle of Britain Historical Society: www.battleofbritain1940.net

Battle of Britain, 13 Group, RAF website: www.raf.mod.uk/bob1940/13group

Caribbean Aircrew in RAF during WW2: www.caribbeanaircrew-ww2.com

Clydebank Blitz, Tom Kendrick: www.tommckendrick.com

Feldgrau – Research on German Armed Forces: www.feldgrau.com

Luftwaffe in Norway, Special Interest Group: www.luftwaffe.no/bilde2.html

Luftwaffe Archives & Records Resource Group: www.lwag.org

Luftwaffe Data: luftwaffedata.co.uk

Luftwaffe, 1933–1945: www.ww2.dk

Naval History: www.naval-history.net

Secret Scotland: www.secretscotland.org.uk

Twelve O'clock High: forum.12oclockhigh.net

U-Boat Net: uboat.net

Wartime Memories Project: www.wartimememories.co.uk

Wekusta: www.warcovers.dk

Wings Over Wick: www.caithness.org/wings

World War Two Airfields & Radar Stations: worldwar2airfields.fotopic.net

WW2 in Color Forum: www.ww2incolor.com

# Index